M000218339

"For anyone wh [...] al or physical abuse, the promise of this book can seem impossible. Yet I urge you to pick up this book and read just the first few chapters. You'll end up reading it all yourself, like I did, and thinking of a dozen people who need to read it as well. The honesty, insights, and spiritual truth that come from these reality-soaked stories show that chains really can be broken. Love, hope, freedom, and the ability to build healthy relationships can be yours—even if you've come from the most broken, difficult background. And if you work, live, or minister to people who carry these chains— you must read this book."

—JOHN TRENT, PhD, president,
The Center for StrongFamilies and StrongFamilies.com
author of *The Blessing* and *The 2 Degree Difference*

"*Breaking Invisible Chains* reveals the agonizing reality of emotional pain while pointing people to healing and hope. I highly recommend this book!"

—CAROL KENT, speaker and author of *When I Lay My Isaac Down*
and *Between a Rock and a Grace Place*

"It's never easy to talk about domestic abuse. That's why it's important to read true stories like these and meet real women who felt trapped with nowhere to turn. They are here to tell you those chains can be broken. If you are silently suffering, this book will show you the way out. If you know someone in an abusive situation, this book will give you the courage to speak the truth in love. With God's compassion as their guide, each author and contributor offers practical advice and genuine hope."

—LIZ CURTIS HIGGS, best-selling author of *Bad Girls of the Bible*

Other New Hope books by
Susan Titus Osborn, Jeenie Gordon, Karen Kosman

*Wounded by Words: Healing the Invisible
Scars of Emotional Abuse*

*Too Soon to Say Goodbye: Healing and
Hope for Victims and Survivors of Suicide*

The Way to
Freedom from
Domestic Abuse

breaking
INVISIBLE
chains

Susan Titus Osborn, MA
Jeenie Gordon, MS, MA, LMFT
Karen Kosman

NEW HOPE
PUBLISHERS
Gospel-Centered. Missions-Driven.

BIRMINGHAM, ALABAMA

New Hope® Publishers
P. O. Box 12065
Birmingham, AL 35202-2065

NewHopeDigital.com
New Hope Publishers is a division of WMU®.

Library of Congress Product Control Number: 2013943702

Interior Design: Glynese Northam

ISBN-10: 1-59669-386-X
ISBN-13: 978-1-59669-386-9
N134127 • 0813 • 3M1

Table of Contents

To the outside world a person suffering from emotional hurts usually appears normal and happy. It would be much too shameful to admit to family and friends that abuse was occurring. It is much harder, however, for victims to keep their secrets from their own children, who often suffer in silence.

A newlywed looks forward to a happy marriage, filled with romance. She believes the fairy tale that they will live happily ever after. But in some marital relationships, the dark shadow of abuse begins within the first year, and gradually escalates.

"I promise to love, honor, and cherish" are beautiful words spoken in a wedding ceremony—words said in love that have now dissolved into doubt and regret. Abuse escalates over time. Dreams crumble into a nightmarish existence.

The victim becomes more and more fearful of her mate or boyfriend. As abuse increases, so does fear. Like a smothering blanket, it suffocates, isolates, and dominates. Fear imprisons and overpowers the person's ability to think rationally.

deserve the abuse and are often frozen in an unhealthy state as the result of cruel mistreatment. And unfortunately, many still want to protect their abuser.

God has promised that the truth will set us free. The victim vows to have no more secrets and not to put up with any more abuse. She finally faces the truth and admits what is happening in her life. With the help and advice of a Christian therapist, a minister, family member, or a friend, she vows to change her circumstances.

The abused woman begins the road to restoration. She may turn to a shelter that offers a safe place for victims of domestic abuse—a place where hopes are renewed. She may go to counseling and find the freedom to express hidden fears. She begins to put her life back together through friends, family members, specialists, and a restored faith in the Lord.

The victim learns to get on with her life. God has removed the chains of domestic abuse, freeing her to live again. She is no longer fearful or worried. Home once more becomes a safe, peaceful place. Each day brings a new opportunity for her to attend classes, find a new job, renew friendships, and embrace a closer relationship with the Lord.

Acknowledgments

WE WOULD LIKE to thank Lieutenant Tom Tarpley, Special Operations Division commander, Tustin, California, Police Department for his valuable expertise and input for this book. We would also like to thank the 22 authors who contributed stories regarding their own experiences or the experiences of their clients. Many of the names in the stories and of the authors have been changed. Without the input of these valuable people, this book could not have been written.

Dedication

THIS BOOK IS dedicated to those individuals who have suffered from emotional hurts, verbal and physical abuse, and domestic violence. May they find hope, wholeness, and peace in our Lord Jesus Christ through the pages of this book.

Introduction

EMOTIONAL HURTS AND domestic abuse can happen to anyone. They occur in all age ranges, ethnic backgrounds, and economic levels. It happens to ordinary women who dared to love, but later discovered that the man they married was completely different from the man who courted them. Over time, an abusive partner strips these women of their self-esteem as the darker side of their spouses or boyfriends becomes more evident. This can lead to anxiety and depression and make the victims feel helpless and alone. As the years go by, their abusers belittle and sometimes beat them to the point of threatening their lives.

This mistreatment usually takes place behind closed doors, so we often aren't aware of its existence. However, if we look closer, we will see that abuse happens in our towns, our neighborhoods, even next door, and perhaps among those in our churches.

Yet the problem is often overlooked, denied, or excused. This is especially true when the abuse is verbal or emotional, rather than physical. Psychological abuse is often minimized, yet it can leave lasting, unseen scars. And often emotional abuse escalates into physical and sexual violence.

The National Institute of Justice estimates that in the US one in four women (25 percent) has experienced domestic violence in her lifetime. It is also estimated that up to 6 million women are victims of domestic violence each year. Since many of these instances go unreported, it is difficult to get an accurate count.

Abuse is used for one purpose and one purpose only: to gain and maintain total control over the victim. The abuser may use fear, intimidation, guilt, and shame to wear the person down and keep her or him under his or her control. Although women are more often the victims, men are also abused—usually emotionally and verbally.

The bottom line is that domestic abuse is never acceptable, whether it's coming from a man, a woman, or a teenager. Children and teens are often abused. It's called bullying, and all too often it is considered acceptable behavior. If you recognize someone you know in this description, do not hesitate to reach out. There is help available, and everyone deserves to feel safe, valued, and respected.

Included in this book are stories from men and women who have been victims of domestic abuse and have learned to reconstruct their lives and have found healing by discovering God's peace. Scripture references enlighten the reader to the power of God's grace, love, and mercy to heal shattered lives.

How many women call abuse by its rightful name and make it a question rather than a declaration? Some minimize and justify it.

Because an abuser promises, often in tears, to "never do it again," victims of abuse want to believe their partners' promises and simply want the abuse to stop—but not the relationship to end. Yet the abuse repeats. The signs are subtle and often hard to detect. Victims tend not to tell family, friends, or co-workers. Rather they suffer in silence. Wanting to keep the peace and believing what the abuser is telling them—that they are to blame and deserve the abuse—guilt and shame raise their ugly heads and deter disclosure and honesty.

Reliable sources on domestic violence estimate that, every nine seconds in the US, a woman is assaulted or beaten. And even though abuse will impact an individual's life for many years, it does not need to prevent someone from having a fulfilled and quality life. Hope and healing are possible.

In this book, we deal with how abuse looks. We explain the common characteristics of abuse and abusers. Abusers tend to have similar traits that *are* recognizable, if we begin to identify risk factors and common indicators.

As authors who have all experienced domestic abuse, we are dedicated to the task of providing hope and emotional healing for those who have suffered at the hands of another. And Jeenie, a marriage and family therapist who has counseled numerous abused clients, will share her personal and professional insights.

Our desire is that this book will provide encouragement and suggestions to overcome what seems to be a hopeless situation. Our prayer is that this book will bring understanding, hope, and healing—that lives will be saved.

"My father, a medical doctor, and my mother verbally and emotionally abused me throughout my childhood. I was made to feel no good, unable to do anything, and married a man who continued the abuse. Through a Christian therapist, I have dealt with my childhood issues, forgiven my parents, and moved on to wholeness."

—BEVERLY

CHAPTER 1

The Ugly Face
of Hopelessness

You are my hiding place;
you will protect me from trouble
and surround me with songs of deliverance.

—PSALM 32:7

HEARTS CRY SOFTLY, quietly, unnoticed. The silence of the lips keeps the secret—hidden and underground. Embarrassment shuts off any cry for help. Cover-ups, pretending, protecting the abuser—for fear of retribution—becomes the lifestyle. It would be much too shameful to admit to family and friends that abuse was occurring. They would ask questions—ones that have no answers. Undoubtedly they would give suggestions, trying to be helpful but seldom having any real idea of the danger and magnitude of what is going on inside a family, one that looks so right to the outside world. It is much less complicated and far easier to go on pretending and smiling while keeping the horrid secret inside.

It is much easier, however, for victims to keep the abuser's secrets from the outside world than it is to keep them from their own children. Whether children themselves are physically abused or not, they are greatly affected by the abuse—emotional, verbal, and physical—that goes on in their homes.

In the following story, Jeenie shows the effect her father's abuse, both emotional and physical, had on the entire family.

PAPA WAS A PREACHER
JEENIE GORDON

Daddy was a good one—a preacher, that is. People had confidence and faith in him. After all, he was a man of God. He prayed fervently with exuberance and sincerity, and all who heard him thought him exemplary.

One warm summer night in July, when I was only four years old, I knelt at the altar after my father's sermon and asked Jesus to be my Savior. I had the assurance that my heart was changed. It was permanent, and I have continued to love and serve the Lord all my life.

For all of Daddy's spiritual traits, there was sometimes a very different side at home. "Hey kids, grab a spoon." Hurriedly we crammed our little bodies against the table as he plopped down a carton of ice cream. Pastoring did not pay well, so getting a half-gallon of ice cream was an enormous treat. Excitedly three little preschoolers dug into the delicacy, anxious to enjoy the sweet creamy treat, only to find out it was a container of lard. Daddy thought it was funny and, of course, did not produce the real thing.

Many nights, I lay trembling in my bed as I heard my mother and father fighting. Daddy broke furniture, while Mom screamed. I was too young to protect her, so I lay quietly in my bed, hoping my younger brother and sister would sleep through the commotion. Even though Daddy had never physically abused me, I feared it could occur.

After this went on for several years, one day I watched a policeman's blue hat bobbing up and down outside the living room windows as he walked to the back of our house. He took my father to the police car, removing him from our home. In my mind's eye, I vividly remember my four-year-old brother hanging onto Daddy and screaming in emotional pain as the police officer gently closed the door of the patrol car. A divorce ensued.

Seldom did we see our father over the years, as he moved out of state and later remarried. In adulthood, we visited him several times, and I came to realize he did not respect women. As my sister and I developed into maturity, he was caustic, unkind, and cruel in his remarks to us.

Mom never spoke of the spousal abuse, nor did we siblings. She evidently told her immediate birth family, and I suspect they encouraged her to leave the marriage. Many questions remain unanswered, as our heavenly Father chose to take Mom to be with Him.

Abuse crosses all lines: cultural, social, economic, ethnic, educational, and religious. From CEOs in expensive suits to blue-collar workers, abuse knows no boundaries. How could trusted people such as pastors, doctors, police officers, or family members—ones we expect to exhibit high standards and values—act in such evil ways? Sadly, it's because they are people, who often have suffered abuse themselves as children. It can be a learned behavior and carried into adulthood. Unfortunately the chain of abuse often continues through generations. But it is a chosen behavior.

⤙ WORDS FROM JEENIE ⤚

It should be noted: Countless individuals who were abused as children never perpetrate abuse as they mature. They choose not to act out anger, frustration, and their insecurity on unprotected, inferior family members.

If an abuser can be gracious and kind to others outside the home—and they often are—it stands to reason they have the ability to control themselves with their families. There are numerous help organizations available such as counseling, anger management courses, and support groups, etc. However, the only person who can stop the abuse is the abuser

Often abusers hate their actions but refuse to take the necessary steps to change because it is a difficult, slow, and long journey. Thus, they choose the path of least resistance and give in to their practiced aberrant emotions and maltreatment.

Blame is often used against victims. "If you did what I asked and obeyed me instantly, then I would not have treated you this way." Or, "You're the one who gets me so mad. It's all your fault." Or, "You brought this on yourself." The abuser really believes he has no other choice. However, it is important to remember that the abuser makes a conscious choice to abuse the victim. Domestic abuse is targeted, choice-based behavior.

Unfortunately, the victims of abuse often come to believe the abuser's lies, and no matter how hard they try, their situation never seems to change. They wrongly see themselves at fault.

Their families cower in fear and suffer victimization, sometimes believing they can stop the abuse, thinking it will change if they can just become better. However, it is the abuser's choice to change behavior.

Karen felt so warm and secure when Daddy read a bedtime story to her every night. Slowly but surely that security crumbled, and Daddy no longer called her "Little Princess."

LITTLE PRINCESS
KAREN L. KOSMAN

When I was four years old, Daddy and I had a special routine.

After my bubble bath, I would hide under my covers, knowing Daddy would come and read me a story. When I felt him sit down on my bed, I threw off my covers and giggled.

"Hello, Little Princess," Daddy said as he tickled me. "What would you like me to read to you tonight?

"My favorite story," I replied.

Daddy picked up my book and began to read, "Twinkle, twinkle little star."

When Daddy finished reading, I asked, "Why are the stars so far away?"

"Would you like them to be closer?"

"Can you make them come closer?"

"No, but someday, I'll paint stars on your ceiling and make them sparkle."

I threw my arms around Daddy's neck and hugged him.

"Go to sleep now, Princess," he whispered.

Mommy came in and kissed me goodnight. She looked sad.

"Mommy," I asked, "why do you look unhappy?"

"I'm just tired, Karen. Goodnight, see you in the morning."

Several hours later Mommy and Daddy's angry voices woke me up. I wanted to run out and stop them, but was afraid to leave my bed. Soon they stopped. Sleep finally whisked me away to safe hide-away dreams.

In the morning I smelled bacon cooking. I jumped out of bed and ran into the kitchen. We always ate breakfast together on Saturdays. It was one of my favorite times. Mommy stood at the stove mixing scrambled eggs. I looked around for Daddy, but he wasn't there. "Mommy, where's Daddy?"

"He'll be back later," Mommy replied. I noticed tears in her eyes. "Why are you crying?

"I'm not crying, Karen. I just have something in my eye."

Later, my friend Joanie and I helped make cookies. We scooped the dough onto cookie sheets and stuffed our mouths full of chocolate chips. Then we ran off to play in my room with our dolls.

Suddenly, we heard our front door burst open, followed by a cacophony of voices. Daddy yelled, "I don't care what you think, Louise."

Joanie looked up startled and said, "I have to go home now."

Later that night Joanie's parents came over. I didn't understand why I had to go to my room. With my door ajar I heard Joanie's dad say, "Joanie can't play over here anymore." Tears brimmed in my eyes as I thought, *I must have done something bad.*

Their voices grew louder. "Because you're a drunk!" I didn't understand what drunk meant. Then I heard their footsteps going down our front porch steps. My bedroom door opened, and Mommy came into my room and sat down on my bed. She couldn't conceal her tears. I snuggled up to her and asked, "What does drunk mean?"

"Karen, it means your daddy drinks too much wine."

"Why?"

"I don't know, Karen, and I'm not sure what to do."

Things continued to change at home after that incident. Daddy stopped reading me bedtime stories. "Daddy is working hard and comes home too late," is the only explanation Mommy gave.

On the nights he came home early, it seemed like a stranger had replaced my daddy. This stranger looked like my daddy, but he smelled funny, talked with a slur, and staggered when he walked. My love for him gradually turned to fear. A little girl shouldn't have to grieve for her daddy while he's still alive. But, my heart grieved and my mind struggled with questions I feared to ask. After my baby brother, Richard, was born we moved into a bigger house. For a while, things got better. I loved my new bedroom, with its rose-colored walls and wallpaper on one end covered with roses. My closet had a light in it, and I made it into a room for my baby dolls.

My newfound happiness ended after my parents bought their own business. Although I knew she didn't want to, Mom had to go to work every day. We had a fulltime babysitter, but I took on the responsibility to protect my baby brother. Friends often commented to Mom, "Karen is such a mature girl. You must be very proud of her." They didn't understand that outwardly I looked fine, but inwardly a little girl cried.

The nights Daddy came home drunk and yelled at Mommy, I picked up Richard, and we'd hide in my closet. He thought we were playing hide and seek. I liked the nights Daddy came home late. Richard would be asleep in his crib. If I heard loud voices I'd tiptoe into Richard's room and make sure he was OK. Then I'd go hide in my closet.

When everything calmed down I'd go to bed. Often I stared at my ceiling and wondered, *Will Daddy ever paint stars on my ceiling?*

⮜ WORDS FROM JEENIE ⮞

Such precious preschool memories Karen has of her time with Daddy reading a nightly bedtime story, being hugged and loved. Because of these intense emotional feelings, it was impossible to wrap her little mind around a different daddy. Her dream began to fall apart and evaporate when she noticed Mommy crying as well as Daddy smelling funny, his absences, and him no longer reading to his little princess.

Drunk is a harsh, disconcerting word. A bit of light began to dawn on Karen when she understood its meaning. More insight came when her neighbor friend could no longer play with her. Even though it was unfounded, as a little girl, she was certain she had done something bad and was being punished. She no longer had her playmate.

As her daddy's absences grew more frequent, her mother tried to brush away reality—from herself and her children. By making excuses for her husband's heavy work schedule, she was actually enabling his behavior. However, children possess great intuition to sense when all is not right.

When mother needed to work in the business, a babysitter was hired. Yet, Karen felt a responsibility to look after little Richard, to protect and keep him safe. In many children's minds, small places appear to be secure, protected, and a haven of shelter. Thus, a closet certainly fits that description. When her father arrived home drunk late at night, the chaos began, and Karen made certain her baby brother was safe in his crib, then headed for her place of refuge.

Even though two little frightened children may not have known: *God is our refuge and strength, and ever-present help in trouble* (Psalm 46:1),—He was.

As Karen grew older, she became more aware of what was going on between her mother and father. She became traumatized due to the abuse her father inflicted on her mother. One afternoon she tried to escape—literally.

BACKYARD ESCAPE
KAREN L. KOSMAN

One sunny afternoon I was happily playing in our backyard with my best friend, Sharon. Suddenly, we heard a door slam inside the house. I felt my heart skip a beat, and I said, "Sharon, I have to do my homework now. You'd better go home."

"Yes, I need to go do my homework, too. And Dad said we could have pizza tonight."

Even at the tender age of ten, I worried about friends witnessing the ugliness that happened in our house. I watched my friend open the gate and run down our driveway. I sat at our picnic table, wondering if I should go inside, but fear kept me frozen to the bench. Then I heard shouting.

My mind flashed back to the previous night when Dad and Mom had gone out. They'd taken separate cars because Mom wanted to come home early.

Our fulltime daycare provider, Janice, stayed late. She'd do that occasionally as long as my parents reassured her it wouldn't be too late. After my bath I sat in the living room and watched TV. My brother, Richard, and my sister, Diane, had already been tucked in bed. Our new baby brother, Roy, slept soundly in his bassinet. After my show was over, I went to my room and sat on my bed, playing with my dolls until I fell asleep.

I was awakened by Dad shouting Mom's name. "Louise, Louise, *Louise!*" He sounded mad.

"She's not here," Janice replied.

"Why not?" Dad questioned. "She left hours ago."

"All I know is I can't baby-sit at night anymore, if she's not going to keep her promise and come home earlier. It's midnight."

The front door slammed, and I heard Janice's car start up. I thought, *I guess, we'll have a new babysitter soon.* This had happened numerous times.

I tiptoed out of my bedroom and ran across the hall to my brothers' bedroom. When I saw Dad stagger up the hall, I called after him. "Daddy."

"What are you doing up?"

"I'm worried about Mommy. What if she got in an accident?"

"She's OK. Go back to bed."

As I headed for my room, I mumbled under my breath, "You're drunk again." I didn't think I said it loud enough for him to hear, but he swirled around and charged at me. I ran into my brothers' bedroom again and backed up until my body pressed against the wall.

Dad stood in front of me, shouting, "Don't you talk disrespectful to me!" He raised his hand above his head.

I started to cry and whispered, "Don't hit me, Daddy."

We heard the front door open, "Mommy's home," I shouted and darted around Dad. I ran down the hall and threw my arms around her. "I was so scared you'd been in an accident."

"No, but I did get lost. I'm sorry, Karen." Mom took me to my room and tucked me into bed. "You came home just in time. I thought Daddy was going to hit me."

"Why would you think that?"

"Because I mumbled he was drunk. He heard me and got mad. I thought he'd hit me like he did you the other night."

"Karen, I made him mad. That's why he hit me."

"I have a tummy ache. Do I have to go to school tomorrow?"

"Maybe you'll feel better in the morning. Go to sleep now."

Back in the present I felt a cold, wet tongue licking my hand. "Sandy," I whispered, and hugged my Scotty dog, "you're such a good boy. Look, Sandy, I can climb higher in our apricot tree—just like Tarzan."

Another door slammed, and I heard the door to our kitchen porch open. "If you won't go with me, Louise, I'll go alone."

"I'm not going!" Mom shouted after him.

I couldn't listen anymore. Quickly I climbed down from the tree and ran to the wall at the back of our yard. I pulled myself up and over. I knew the yards behind our house intimately. Each fence I climbed took me farther away and made me feel safer. I wanted to keep running forever.

When I was four houses away, I finally stopped running and sat down behind a huge bush. I was breathing hard, but I felt safe—for a little while anyway. I'd stay out long enough to make sure Dad had left, and then I'd sneak back home.

For years, even into my adulthood during times of stress, I dreamt about climbing fences—trying desperately to escape. Then during counseling, my counselor gave me a new image: Jesus helping me down from the fence, holding me, and bringing comfort to my child's heart.

⤚ WORDS FROM JEENIE ⤜

"Well, we fight, but it doesn't bother our children. Usually they're in another room and hear nothing," state many of my clients. I think, *Not so!* As a therapist, I explain to them that little ears are always open. Not only do they hear, but it enters their tender child hearts. Fear grips them in its ugly clutches. They have unanswered questions, "Are my parents going to divorce?" Children are very aware of what divorce looks like and the havoc it plays: going from home-to-home, parental tirades, parents' new friends of the opposite sex, and insecurity because they observe it in their classrooms.

As with little Karen, fear freezes, immobilizes, and threatens youngsters. They walk on eggshells, never knowing what to expect when the abusing parent comes through the front door. Will they be: Drunk or sober? Happy or furious?

Hiding is always a good option for a child. Kids learn that leaving and making themselves scarce works. However, what works for kids does not necessarily work for adults. Too often these habits that play havoc in an adult's life are displayed by an unwillingness to talk through issues. The person may run away, ignore the situation, or completely shut down. They can go from partner-to-partner, job-to-job, friend-to-friend because issues are too overwhelming and difficult to face. They learn someone—like the abuser—is always in control, and thus, they have no rights. Therefore, they disappear.

The protection of her little brothers and sister was of great concern to Karen. She felt as though she was responsible to take care of them. Shield them. As a child, Karen, was unable to do much of anything, but she tried desperately.

Her mother had her own issues of victimization: "Karen, I made Daddy mad. That's why he hit me." Not only did Karen feel a need to look out for her siblings, but also Mom.

Sadly, this type of situation can build into an adult the neurotic need to help everyone, rescue them, and make everything alright They can, and often do, try to take care of others while neglecting their own needs, desires, dreams, and life. They are over-giving, too much and too often. Feeling overly responsible for the well-being of others is referred to in psychological circles as enmeshment, taking on another's issues as your own. It goes far beyond the normalcy of being kind, loving, and caring.

When Karen told her brother she was writing a book on domestic abuse, he opened up and told her his story.

FINALLY ABLE TO SPEAK THE TRUTH
RICHARD STOKES

The night before my eldest sister, Karen, left to join her husband in Germany she hugged each of us and said, "Take care of Mom."

I took those words to heart and vowed to be Mom's protector. Life in our home was like sitting inside a volcano . . . waiting . . . waiting for the next eruption. I overheard Mom tell Dad, "Please, get help for your drinking before it's too late."

He just stared at her and replied, "I don't need any help."

As I watched him walk away, I felt rage growing within me. I often wondered why he loved the booze more than his family. He was intelligent and had his own successful business. We lived in a beautiful home and had nice cars, but we didn't have any emotional security.

Night, after night, the other kids and I would eat dinner with Mom, not knowing when Dad would show up. Almost every night he came home late, already a bit inebriated. He flopped down in front of TV while Mom prepared a steak for his dinner. No matter what she cooked for the rest of the family, when he finally showed up, she cooked him a steak.

"Milt," Mom would call, "your dinner is on the table." Without a word Dad would stand and walk into the kitchen. On one of those routine evenings, Dad's abuse started to escalate. To this day, I'm not sure what began the argument, but we heard Mom crying and Dad yelling. I charged into the dining room just in time to see him shove her. I quickly stepped in front of her.

"Dad, stop!" I yelled. I don't know what I thought I could do at 13 years old, but there I stood. Dad glared at me. He doubled his hand into a fist and said, "I've been waiting for this."

Next thing I knew his fist slammed into my body, and I found myself sprawled out on the dining room floor. I heard Mom cry out, "Richard. Oh no! Richard, are you OK?"

"I'm OK." I gritted my teeth ready to get up and fight. Dad took a step towards me. Then he suddenly stopped and walked away. "No matter what," I mumbled, "he's not going to hurt Mom ever again." I realized that within the past year things at home had gotten worse—much worse.

Later, I lay awake, still too upset to sleep. My mind flashed back a couple of years to when I was in grammar school. I'd always struggled with my reading. My teacher, Mr. Ore, volunteered to come to our house and tutor me. "That's good, Richard," he'd always say after a lesson.

I really felt like my reading was improving—until a few fatal afternoons when Dad came home early—drunk. He staggered over to where Mr. Ore and I were studying and said to my teacher, "You can leave now."

Each time I wanted to disappear. Mr. Ore looked at me and smiled. I know he was trying to reassure me, but I didn't care anymore. Anger raged through my mind.

Dad, if you don't care about me reading, then it must be because you think I've failed. You're way of teaching me to read has always been to knock me in the back of the head. So why am I trying?

I didn't expect an answer to my question, but it came a few minutes later. My bedroom was next to our den, and I heard Dad crying, and yes, praying, "I messed up again. Please help me, Lord. I can't seem to help myself."

Tears sprang to my eyes as I listened to Dad. I loved him, but I didn't understand him. When he was sober, he was a different person. When he was drunk and abusive, I vowed to continue to defend Mom. Then a few years later, I once again, stood between Mom and Dad. This time he hit me so hard I fell against the fireplace and cut my head. My brother, Roy, and his girlfriend came running into the living room to help.

Soon after that, Mom announced to each of us "I'm leaving your dad. I found an apartment and a job for a plumbing company. We're going to move. I'm not telling your dad anything." It was the saddest day of my life, but it was also the happiest.

I am now a senior citizen, and all these years I never shared my pain. I suppressed it, like so many do. Then something special happened. While I was in the hospital after having a heart attack, God whispered to me, *Son, find your faith.*

I found a home church after that experience. I realize now that my gift for a good sense of humor came from God. My determination to succeed in life came from God. I know I still have a ways to go in my Christian walk, but it's a beginning. I am excited to experience life as His plan unfolds for me on a daily basis. I am starting to understand that in God I have a Father who will not abandon me. This has helped me to forgive my dad and move on.

☙ WORDS FROM JEENIE ❧

Richard's father was like many others in believing he needed no help for his drinking. When alcohol is involved in the abuse, the abuser tends to exacerbate the extent of the abuse by exerting more power and control over the victim.

One prevailing myth about domestic violence is that alcohol and drugs are the major causes of domestic abuse. In reality, *some* abusers rely on substance use (and abuse) as an excuse for becoming violent. Researchers find that alcohol allows the abuser to justify his abusive behavior as a result of the alcohol, however, an abuser does not become violent "because" drinking causes him to lose control of his temper. Physical violence is used to exert power and control over another; it does not represent a loss of control.

Continual behavior?

It's interesting how Mom always made her husband a special steak for dinner. Dad had a sense of entitlement, "I deserve the best." And she gave it to him. The belief that one deserves to do and say anything they choose gives credence to abuse. These individuals are often self-centered, controlling, and all-knowing.

A young, skinny teenage boy was so angry and protective of his mom, he felt he needed to take his dad on. Not realizing he could not physically nor emotionally stand up to his father, he was pummeled. Yet, courageously, Richard tried again several years later—all to no avail. Even if teens can stand up to an adult physically, they are emotionally immature, tender, and vulnerable. They are no match for an abuser.

Kids in abusive homes often give up. They stop trying, as Richard did when his father berated his inability to read well. Yet, later in life Richard realized he had a good sense of humor and chose to make positive decisions in order to succeed. As a result, he reached his goals.

It's common for abusers at times to feel badly, particularly when they are sober. Often they cry, ask for forgiveness, and make promises to their families as well as to God, just as Richard's father did.

Even when abuse has been going on for years, there is both joy and sadness when the perpetrator leaves. Although there is relief because the abuse is over, an emotionally painful separation often occurs.

Over and over I see emotional turmoil when a wife leaves the home, when children go out on their own to get away from the constant turmoil, or when a girl realizes her abusing boyfriend has dumped her. Letting go is not easy. Even more difficult is facing the truth about the abuser.

Our heads say one thing—our emotions another. So often, professional help is needed to move toward wholeness.

PSALM 59: 16– 17

But I will sing of your strength,
in the morning I will sing of your love;
for you are my fortress,
my refuge in times of trouble.

You are my strength, I sing praise to you;
you, God, are my fortress,
my God on whom I can rely.

Living in an abusive home often causes children to feel responsible for their moms and/or their younger siblings. In their own strength, they are unable to stand up to the abusive person in their family.

However the Lord has promised to love us and to provide His strength for those who hope in Him. As the psalmist says: *For you are my fortress, my refuge in times of trouble.*

REFLECTION: Looking back on your childhood, do you see a time when you may have experienced verbal, emotional, physical, or sexual abuse?

PRAYER: *Lord, at times, we find ourselves in a situation we have no control over. When we are afraid, please be our refuge and protect us. Allow your peace to fill our hearts and minds. In Jesus' name we pray, amen.*

"He was controlling. Every telephone call and letter received/written was scrutinized. There was no freedom to see family or friends. The put-downs, anger, constant infidelities, and emotional abuse scarred me. In time, I was able to get free."

—ELIZABETH

CHAPTER 2

We've Only Just Begun

*For I know the plans I have for you," declares the
LORD, "plans to prosper you and not to harm you,
plans to give you hope and a future.*

—JEREMIAH 29:11

DO YOU REMEMBER where you were on May 18, 1980, at
8:32 A.M. PDT? It is a day that has gone down in history—a
day that started out routinely for many people. Shock waves
reached across the continent as news came through the media
of a volcanic eruption in the state of Washington. Mount Saint
Helens had literally blown her top.

Over the years many tourists had visited this majestic
mountain whose snow-clad peak reached 9,677 feet. Also
many people built their homes on this beautiful mountain.
Although it was known to be an active volcano, they didn't
worry because it had last erupted in 1857. Nevertheless,
the local government created plans for a safe evacuation of
surrounding towns and mountain homes if needed.

Scientists used equipment to study the activities deep
within this mysterious mountain. In March of 1980 the
scientific community took notice when literally hundreds of
earthquakes occurred on Mount Saint Helens.

Then on the morning of May 18, 1980, a massive avalanche was triggered by an earthquake measuring 5.1 on the Richter scale. An eruption resulted, reducing the elevation of the mountain's summit from 9,677 feet to 8,365 feet. The top was replaced with a one-mile-wide horseshoe-shaped crater. A sudden surge of magma from the earth's mantle caused the eruption, leading to the deadliest and most destructive volcanic event in the history of the United States.

Within moments the largest landslide in recorded history removed more than 1,300 feet from the summit and swept away almost the entire north side of the mountain. A huge plume of ash and pumice filled the sky. Surrounding forests were reduced to rubble. Homes, businesses, and personal property were destroyed, not to mention the loss of human lives.

Just as pressure builds within a volcano, so does emotional pressure build within an abuser. Misguided emotions churn and bubble in the hearts and minds of those who are abusive—finally exploding in an eruption that sweeps over and harms the people they promise to love.

Domestic abuse destroys homes and lives, creates economic strife, and in some cases causes death.

Sometimes abuse begins shortly after a couple is wed, as Susan sadly discovered.

MY PERFECT MAN
SUSAN TITUS OSBORN

At the age of 18, I fell in love with the man who became my husband three years later. I'll call him Craig. He was thoughtful and caring, and I knew I wanted to spend the rest of my life with this special man. Craig seemed solid as a rock and had his sights on becoming an aeronautical engineer.

We went to the island of Kauai in Hawaii for our honeymoon. During one of our special walks we discovered a secret waterfall with a slide and spent many hours in that secluded location. By nightfall we feasted on mouthwatering Hawaiian delicacies. One evening, the music, hula dancers, and men swinging batons of fire held us spellbound. I looked over at Craig and thought, *I am floating on clouds with my perfect man on our perfect honeymoon.*

Then the unexpected happened. One morning while Craig was sleeping, I reached over and brushed his cheek. Without warning, he grabbed me and threw me across the room, severely bruising my leg. I crawled to a chair directly across from our bed, sat down, and burst into tears—my heart shattered.

Craig appeared to me to awake, and then said, "Susan, what's wrong? Why are you crying?"

"You don't remember throwing me across the room?"

He replied, "I'm sorry, Susan. I grew up sharing a bedroom with my brother, and we were always roughhousing like that. I certainly didn't mean to hurt you."

I accepted his apology, but I was still shaking. I couldn't help but wonder if he really had no memory of what he'd just done. My dreams of cuddling with my perfect man dissolved, and I made sure I never touched him again when he was asleep.

Three years later, we had a son, Richard, and two years after that, Michael was born. I had my hands full with a toddler and a newborn baby. Craig was a good breadwinner, but he seemed to have little time to help with the boys. Then one evening he announced, "Susan, we need to get away as a family. I think we should go camping on the weekends."

"That's a wonderful idea," I replied. "It will be a little challenging to take a three-month-old baby camping, though."

"I'll buy a trailer." Within a month after that conversation, he bought an old Aljo camping trailer and fixed it up. Then we pulled it out to the Colorado River one Friday afternoon.

I was really excited to get out of the house and enjoy time with friends. Saturday night, I settled the boys in their bunk bed, which I had tied up with playpen webbing so they would not fall out. They went to sleep immediately after spending the day on the beach under an umbrella.

When we went outside, our friend Paul shouted, "Hey, you two, come join us."

A group of our friends were playing board games by the campfire, and I hurried over. "How fun! Actually this is the first time since Michael was born that I've been able to visit with all of you."

About ten o'clock, my husband said, "Let's go to bed. I want to get up and water-ski early in the morning."

I felt so disappointed. "I'm having so much fun. I'm not tired, and this is the first time I've spent an evening with friends in I don't know how long."

"No! We're going to bed," he demanded.

Embarrassed that he'd carry on like that in front of our friends, I stood up and followed him over to our trailer. With a heavy heart I tried appealing to his sensitive side. "Please, let me stay up for a while, even if you go to bed."

Rage filled his face, and he turned around and hit me. I reeled back, my head spinning. Neither one of us said another word. We quietly went into the trailer and went to bed.

The next morning I had a swollen, black eye. I anticipated that he'd at least apologize, but he acted like nothing had happened.

I felt ashamed and thought, *I can't tell anyone what really happened.* When we came out of the trailer, with everyone staring at me, I stammered, "I ran into the trailer door last night." But I could tell by their facial expressions that no one believed me.

At this point I just wanted to leave, to get away from their questioning eyes before I burst into tears.

Once we did return home, heaviness remained on my heart. Every time I looked in our bathroom mirror, my swollen, black eye reminded me of my husband's abuse. I prayed, "Lord, I didn't deserve this treatment. What should I do?"

A few days later, I felt the Lord pressing upon my heart to talk to Craig and take a firm stand. Once the boys were asleep, I sat down on the couch and quietly said, "If you ever lay a hand on me again, this marriage is over."

He replied, "I'm sorry, Susan. I didn't mean to hit you. I don't know what came over me. I will never do it again." And he never did.

However, there are many other forms of spousal abuse, ones that cause hidden scars rather than visible ones. Looking back over the 22 years of my first marriage, I now see that I was the victim of emotional, verbal, and physical abuse.

⮞❧ WORDS FROM JEENIE ❧⮜

Craig's response, after he threw Susan across the room, was lame. Yet, quite typical of an abuser trying to confuse the victim into misinterpreting violent behavior.

Often it's because the victim feels she must keep her marriage intact. Susan loved her husband—the father of her boys—and wanted to keep her marriage.

However, abusive men are controllers, as previously stated. They have unique ways and means and are always coming up with new and creative ideas to maintain control over their partners. Often, after a women gives in to the control, she thinks, *What really just happened?* Of course it's after the fact, and she may swallow it—again.

Embarrassing the victim is a common tool an abuser uses. The husband may not seem to care what others may think about him. He is focused on his wife doing exactly as he asked, without questioning or commenting.

It worked for Craig. Susan dutifully followed him to bed, carrying a heavy heart—suffering in silence. Out of fear, seldom will an abused woman make a scene or refuse the wishes of her husband, especially in the company of others. That's exactly the reason a controller gets by with such inhumane treatment—it works.

Lying is a way a victim may try to protect herself. Even though others do not believe—as it was in Susan's case—other people choose to stay out of the situation. Yet, keeping closed mouths may give a perception of credence to the abuse that should not be kept hidden or excused.

Abuse morphs and escalates throughout the course of a relationship when unaddressed. Verbal accusations, putdowns, screaming, and cursing do increase to physical abuse. Over time, some victims may seem to justify and rationalize the abuser's behavior, yet condemn themselves. This is part of the cycle of control that an abuser uses to his advantage. He may apologize and seem remorseful and promise never to do it again, then blame the victim for her actions when he chooses violence yet again.

Women tend to classify abuse. Some only consider it abuse if they have a black eye, as did Susan. Others believe broken bones are the criteria. Few believe verbal accusations, putdowns, screaming and cursing, or constant controlling is abuse. They often justify and rationalize the behavior, yet condemn themselves.

Mistreatment of any kind is abuse.

Within the female is an enormous need for safety and security. Women stay with abusive men for years, often because the fear of leaving is too strong. And that fear is justifiable. *Where would I go? I have no job skills. What about my little kids? I can't raise them alone? What will people think?* The questions are without number, and there appear to be few if any answers.

Looking into the tear-filled dark eyes of a beautiful young client, I heard her whisper, "I've decided to stay and just try harder." Although she was not married to the man with whom she lived, they have a child. The boyfriend blatantly stated in my office, "I will never marry you." She felt trapped, even though her family urged her to leave.

Because Craig, as he had promised, never again laid a hand on Susan, she assumed the abuse was over. Yet, how wrong she was.

TOTAL CONTROL
SUSAN TITUS OSBORN

Craig kept his promise and never hit me again after that incident at the Colorado River. However, one evening he became very angry, ran into our bedroom, and put his fist through the door. I didn't even know what had upset him. Mike started crying, and I put my arms around him to calm him down. I said, "Let's go into your bedroom and read a bedtime story with Richard.

I read one of their favorite Dr. Seuss books and had them laughing in no time. We said nightly prayers together, and then I prayed silently that the incident the boys had just witnessed would soon be forgotten. Neither one of them ever mentioned it again.

After getting the boys settled in bed, I found my husband sitting in the family room, calmly reading the newspaper, as if nothing had happened.

I confronted him. "Why did you put your fist through the door? Mike was really scared."

Craig put down the newspaper and sighed. "I was really angry with you, Susan. The house was a mess when I came home. The boys had their toys all over the family room. I had a bad day at work and expected to have a relaxing evening at home."

"I'm sorry, Craig. The family room is the only room that has a wood floor for the boys to run their trucks on. They can't run them on carpeting. They were playing up until the time you came home."

"Just be glad I hit the door instead of you, Susan. This conversation is over. I have work to do that I brought home from the office." And with those comments, he got up from the couch, walked into the office, and slammed the door. He never mentioned the incident again.

Several years later, Richard expressed an interest in playing the piano. A friend at church agreed to teach him and suggested that I take lessons too. I found it fun, and it gave me an appreciation for music and for the gifts of perfect pitch and nimble fingers that my oldest son possessed—gifts not given to me.

One day I was practicing my simple little songs when my husband walked in. He listened for a moment and then said, "You play terribly."

"I know," I agreed, and then added, "but I'm really having fun."

"I don't care if you're having fun. I want you to stop the lessons."

"Why? I really enjoy playing—"

He interrupted me midsentence. "It's a waste of your time and my money. End of discussion."

With those words, he stomped out of the living room.

A feeling of overpowering sadness filled my heart. I knew it wasn't a matter of money. He was an executive and made a good salary, and there was always enough money for his golf and flying lessons. I never resented his activities. Yet, he was very controlling, and when he made up his mind about something, no room remained for discussion.

I sighed and closed the piano lid. I put my music in the piano bench and never played again.

⚘ WORDS FROM JEENIE ⚘

What a childish thing to do—Craig putting his fist through the door. This packed an emotional wallop on his wife and little boy. His intention was to show them who was in charge.

It's easy to see Craig's exaggerated control issues, his narcissistic view of life, and his willingness to go to many lengths so that his family would obey without question.

Even while earning an excellent living and spending money on the things he wanted—golfing and flying instruction—he was not willing to pay a nominal fee for Susan's piano lessons. It was not about the money. It was about preventing Susan from doing something she enjoyed. It would be his way and his way only.

Susan thought by giving in to her husband, she could keep peace in her family. However, as time went by, she realized the situation would only become worse.

A DIFFICULT DECISION
SUSAN TITUS OSBORN

By the time the boys were teenagers, the verbal abuse had escalated to a point where my husband was always putting me down and belittling me. I honestly didn't know how to react. Wanting the marriage to last, I did nothing. I *thought* this was a way to keep peace in the family, but I was uninformed.

As time passed, my husband spent more weekends on the East Coast than on the West Coast with us. When I discovered I also had a biblical basis for doing so, I filed for a legal separation.

When I asked my kids if they were comfortable with my decision to seek a divorce, Mike said, "We wish you would've made that decision two years ago, Mom. Do you realize what you have put us through?"

Richard added, "We were losing our respect for you because you always let Dad treat you poorly. And it broke our hearts to watch him make fun of you."

"I'm sorry, boys," I replied. "I had a quarter of a century invested in your dad, and I wanted to try and make things work."

Richard said, "It takes two to make a marriage, Mom, and Dad quit a long time ago."

I realized that my wise son was right. The changes in my husband's behavior toward me were so subtle over a long period of time that I didn't see how the relationship had changed. I felt like the boys and I had suffered from deep emotional scars because of my lack of action.

I asked the boys to forgive me for what they went through, and I have forgiven my ex-husband for the way he treated me. Forgiveness has set me free, and after six years of being a single parent, I married a man who cherishes me, encourages me, and supports me in my writing ministry. I thank God every day for this wonderful man, and I pray that the walk I walked, difficult as it was, will benefit others through my words.

It is important to be aware of this pattern, as explained by the authors of *Children's Perspectives on Domestic Violence:*

> Often abusers encourage mothers to see themselves as failures. They drag kids into the abuse and may even turn kids against the mother. Sometimes the mother is too injured or dazed from the abuse to give kids the attention they want and need. In other cases, mothers may comply with the abuser and demean themselves to reduce the amount of violence their children have to see. It's not uncommon for children to blame their mother for not leaving sooner, even if they can understand that the mother stayed for the sake of the children. This is faulty logic to them because they would rather be away from the violence.

WORDS FROM JEENIE

So often after an abused woman has filed for divorce, her teenagers ask, "Why did you wait so long?" as did Susan's sons. Kids are often more up front and real about the situation. They call a spade a spade, while Mom tries to blanket herself and them with pretend security.

The best piece of the story is that Susan has forgiven Craig. Forgiveness is a long time coming—a journey. Fast forgiveness is not real. It's phony. We must travel the road, do our best to deal with the issues, and come to grips with reality prior to forgiving. It is a process.

Forgiving Craig allowed Susan to look closely to see the abuser, the abuse, and herself—what had become of her life.

Then she could work on issues and make changes. It gave her the freedom to love again, marry, and experience true security. Forgiveness sets us free!

Debbie also tried to hold her marriage together, hoping things would change, if she could only jump through the hoops. Unfortunately, her controlling husband kept raising the bar.

I THOUGHT THINGS WOULD CHANGE
DEBBIE WHEELAND

At age 17, I found out I was pregnant. I was so young, but I managed to graduate from high school before saying, "I do." Before we were married, I knew Kenny went out with the boys and drank, but I thought he would change after the wedding. After all, he soon was going to become a father.

Four months later I became a mother, and his drinking and late nights continued to increase as time went on.

I can't remember the first time he raised a fist at me and threatened to hit me.

Was he drunk or sober? He seemed to be angry with me for silly things, like the time the phone rang and he answered, receiving a sudden click. He asked, "Who was that on the phone, your boyfriend?"

I was shocked he would even think that. I replied, "Boyfriend, that's silly. I'm married to you. I don't have a boyfriend."

"You're a liar," he screamed. Little by little I grew more afraid of him.

Often he brought a friend home for his lunch break, and he was always nice when someone else was around. But one time, he came home alone. Grabbing me by the shirt collar, he shoved me into our small kitchen. He opened the cupboards and shouted, "Look at them, you slob. They are filthy. You've never had it so good. You were nothing before you married me. You need to clean up this kitchen before I get home from work tonight."

Trembling I replied, "I'll clean them this afternoon, Kenny. The kitchen will be spotless by the time you come home." I watched his truck pull away. Tears and bitter thoughts filled my mind while I grabbed a dishcloth, dipped it in soapy water, and washed out all the cupboards.

Proud of the job I had accomplished, I took a shower, curled my hair, put on makeup, and dressed in one of Kenny's favorite outfits. I only hoped he would be in a better mood after work.

Hours later after the children were sleeping, I glanced at the clock. *He should have been home hours ago*, I thought with a sigh. The sun had set, the dinner grew cold, and I sat forlorn on another disappointing and lonely night.

Nothing was said when he strolled into the bedroom in the wee hours of the morning. He undressed and tumbled into bed, and I knew he'd been drinking. I pretended to be asleep.

A couple of weeks passed before another incident occurred. I always had a soda and a hearty sandwich ready for him in case he showed up for lunch. However, I never knew when he would bother, and he never gave me any prior warning that he'd come home for lunch.

Then one hot summer day while the kids and I were having a water fight in the backyard with the teenage boys across the alley, Kenny's truck screeched into the driveway.

Walking out back, he saw me dressed in my two-piece bathing suit. I held the telltale hose in my hands and had the water turned on full blast on our kids and the neighbors. They were giggling and scrambling around me.

He eyed the neighbors suspiciously and screamed. "Get in the house now and fix my lunch!"

I looked around, hoping he had come with a co-worker, but he was alone. "Oh, I didn't know you were coming home today. Let me shut off the water, and I will fix you a sandwich."

"Get your butt in here now—and put some clothes on. I know you like parading in front of those teenage boys half naked."

"What do you mean by that?" I asked. "The kids and I were having a water fight with them. Everyone was having fun."

His voice got louder, "I said go change and fix my lunch."

Quickly I ran to the bedroom, praying softly the whole way. "Please, God, convince him I am good. I didn't do anything wrong."

He was unusually quiet while our three young children tried to engage him in conversation. "Daddy, we were having so much fun soaking our friends with our hose. Can you come out and play with us?"

He completely ignored them. The children wolfed down their lunches and headed out to the backyard again. As soon as they were out of sight, he grabbed me by the back of the neck. "Come here and take a look at this." Shoving me toward the long narrow hallway he shouted, "Look at these floor boards. They're filthy. I want you to scrub them until they shine. Looks like you won't have time anymore to play outside with the neighbors." He sneered as he strolled out the front door.

I felt hot tears well up in my eyes and spill over onto my cheeks. My face was red with humiliation, anger, and embarrassment. Peeking through the curtain, I hoped the neighbor kids hadn't heard him yelling at me. I decided to let my children play outside a little longer. I gathered together the cleaning supplies, fell on my knees, and began scrubbing. I sobbed. "What is wrong with me? Why does he treat me this way?"

I didn't want the kids to see me like this. I had to get a hold of myself before they came in the house. Looking heavenward I prayed, "Why, God? I don't understand. I've been a Christian for three years. I thought things were supposed to get better. Why does my husband hate me and treat me with such contempt? I must deserve to be treated this way! Please help me, God!"

WORDS FROM JEENIE

When I was counseling at the high school, I walked through the pregnancy with a beloved 14-year-old freshman. I encouraged her to tell her parents. The next morning she ran into my office and dissolved in a flood of tears. Her parents had thrown her out. Hurriedly I arranged placement for her in a loving, caring facility.

One sunny day, my office phone rang. "Mrs. Gordon, I had my baby girl last night."

Checking on her whereabouts, I arrived with flowers as soon as school was dismissed. Dressed in hospital garb, I entered her room to an excited gasp of pleasure.

"I want you to be the first one to hold my baby," she exclaimed. As I held the precious infant in my arms, thoughts exploded in my mind. *This dear teenager went through birth all alone—no parent in sight.* I wrapped her in my arms and told her how proud I was of her courage. Over the years, I saw her become a wonderful mother, finish high school, and enter college.

Debbie had hoped things would change for the better when they were married and he became a father. She imagined a different life. Therefore, Debbie did her best to please Kenny, to prove her love for him, look attractive, have a well-kept home, have lunch prepared in case he came home unexpectedly, and whatever else she could. She even begged God to help her do the right thing.

In the eyes of Kenny, Debbie always missed the mark. Debbie was amazed that she could never satisfy Kenny, no matter how hard she tried. There is no pleasing a manipulating, controlling, and abusing spouse.

PSALM 121
I lift up my eyes to the mountains—
where does my help come from?
My help comes from the Lord,
the Maker of heaven and earth.

He will not let your foot slip—
he who watches over you will not slumber;
indeed, he who watches over Israel
will neither slumber nor sleep.

The Lord watches over you—
the Lord is your shade at your right hand;
the sun will not harm you by day,
nor the moon by night.

The Lord will keep you from all harm—
he will watch over your life;
the Lord will watch over your coming and going
both now and forevermore.

When we were dating, we looked at the world through rose-colored glasses. We saw the best in our special man, which was easy to do because he was on his finest behavior. Then after we were married, gradually we saw little signs that showed us our relationship was not as perfect as we had imagined. Storm clouds gathered, but we desperately held on, not wanting to see our dreams crushed. Loneliness and anxiety filled our hearts.

Yet remember Psalm 121 states that the Lord is always watching over us, and He does not want us to suffer from abuse or come to any harm. We can count on His promise.

REFLECTION: Have you ever seen—and ignored—red flags in a relationship?

PRAYER: *Lord, send angels to surround me. Help my heart to sort out the truth. My mind screams for a solution, yet my heart whispers that nothing is wrong. Please, protect me and help me to make wise decisions. In Jesus' name we pray, amen.*

❧

"Most of my marriage I had a black eye. Often I went to the emergency room to get help for one injury or another. My counselor found a safe place for my children and me and we no longer live in fear."

—STACY

CHAPTER 3

The Honeymoon Is Over

Husbands, love your wives and do not be harsh with them.

—COLOSSIANS 3:19

SOFT MUSIC, SWEET-SMELLING flowers, glowing candles, and satin bows throughout the church silently promise the fulfillment of dreams. A reverent hush settles over the church as the wedding party enters, followed by a beautiful, but slightly nervous bride. Tears and smiles mingle among the guests, as the bride and groom look lovingly into one another's eyes and vow to love, honor, and cherish—until death do we part.

Women dream of romance and a love that will last long after the glitter of the wedding. Fairy tales with happy endings tell of the prince who whisks away his bride. But real life is not a fairy tale. Many people who marry in today's society no longer treat marriage as a sacred union.

Sadly, some marriages end terribly wrong as one spouse begins to reveal an ugly reality—the need to control, dominate, and abuse the spouse, rather than to love and cherish her forever. The person who promised to love you forever is now your worst nightmare. The truth is, the controlling spouse not only betrays their loved one, but they dishonor God and His purpose for marriage.

Debbie's dream of a fairy-tale marriage dissolved into doubt and regret. Domestic abuse that started out verbally and emotionally escalated into physical violence as well. She hoped things would change, but they didn't, and one day she showed her courage.

I SAW THE LIGHT
DEBBIE WHEELAND

Opening my eyes to the soft light of daylight streaming in through a crack in the lace curtains, I turned and looked at my husband of eight years. I marveled at the serene look on his face while he slept.

Not wanting to wake him, I carefully rolled out of bed and tiptoed out of our bedroom. Alone in the bathroom, I stared at my reflection in the mirror. I winced as I noticed the black-and-blue mark on my cheek. My thoughts churned. *God, it still hurts a little. I should have known not to question him about where he'd been last night.*

I found my eye shadow and dabbed some brown color to try and hide the bluish bruise. It had actually been some time since he had raised a fist to me. *Somehow I must have deserved to be hit*, I thought.

"Please, God," I whispered, "change me. Please convince him I really am a good wife. I try to do all the right things. Please don't let him hit me anymore."

Suddenly, Kenny banged on the bathroom door and screamed, "Are you in there?"

"I'm sorry! I'll be right out."

When I opened the door, he grabbed hold of the doorknob and pushed me aside. The stench of alcohol reeked from his body. Obviously he was still drunk from the night before. But

I was thankful he hadn't noticed my face. I wasn't up for false promises or feigned regrets again.

My mind flashed back a few years to when I became a Christian. I'd rejoiced when Kenny came to church with me and said the salvation prayer. I'd been hopeful that our lives would change. Although Kenny rarely went to church anymore, he hadn't tried to stop the kids and me from going.

Over the next several months our fights were less frequent because I learned to keep my mouth shut during his accusations and rages. That is until Labor Day weekend.

"Deb, wake up," Kenny ordered. "I'm anxious to try out my new lawnmower. You and the kids need to get up and help."

That was our typical routine for the weekend. He controlled every moment of my life. I never made plans of my own—just did what I was told.

After spending a couple of hours raking and stuffing the cut grass inside the trashcans, I was ready for a break.

Unexpectedly, a white car pulled up in our driveway. "Hey, Deb, you want to go to the picnic at church?" My friend Pat inquired.

The mower shut off. Kenny started walking in my direction with a scowl on his face. Quickly I said, "I don't know if Kenny will let me."

"Ask him," Pat said.

Panicking, I pleaded, "Will you ask him?"

"Hi, Kenny. Today is our church picnic. Can Deb and the kids go? It would mean a lot to me. Marlena and I are going to be baptized today." She motioned toward her only child.

"No!" he said abruptly. "She has yard work to finish." Then he turned and walked away.

Stepping out of her car, Pat followed him and said, "Come on, Kenny, why don't you let her go?"

Angrily, he shouted. "Because Deb has work to do, and I said no!" He glanced over at me with a threatening glare.

Cowering, I said, "Sorry, Pat, I guess I can't go."

Over the next year, I experienced a season of growth as I learned to walk closer to Jesus while detaching from Kenny's tirades. Although Kenny hadn't hit me for quite a while, the verbal abuse continued. And whenever he got ready to go out drinking, he'd always start a fight. "Look at this house. It's filthy. You're a lazy slob! I'm going out!"

However, I no longer hurt over Kenny's allegations against me. No longer did I feel the need to defend myself. I felt the Lord comforting me, and I prayed, "You are my defender. Bring truth and justice to me. Protect me from my husband. Bring peace to our home."

On the following Labor Day weekend, I quickly finished my yard work and anxiously waited for Pat to arrive. I hadn't said anything to Kenny, but she and I had made plans to go to the church picnic. I didn't want to be bossed around anymore!

The white car pulled up in the driveway. "Hey, Deb," she called, "are you ready to go to the baptism and picnic?"

"Kenny, can I go to with Pat?"

Strolling over to the car, he leered at me. "No! You have yard work to finish."

"No, I don't! I'm finished," I protested.

"You're not going, and that's that!"

"Yes, I am!" I said.

"Pat, you better leave. She's not going anywhere."

Sadly, Pat backed out of the driveway.

"Why can't I go?" I asked bravely.

"Because I said you can't."

My three kids stopped what they were doing and watched anxiously.

"Well, I am going! Come on, you guys. Wash up. We're going to the picnic."

Suddenly, I felt a sharp pain in my back between my shoulder blades. Then Kenny grabbed my tank top and ripped it down the front. I ran from him as tears flowed down my face. Clutching my hand to my chest, careful to hold my torn shirt, I crossed the yard and headed toward the front door.

Forcefully he grabbed me again, but I quickly pulled away and ran into the house. In an agonizing moment of truth I caught a glimpse of my young children with their mouths agape. I vowed this would be the last time he ever touched me!

I knew I did not deserve to be hit or mistreated by him any longer. At that moment I thought, *Somehow, someway with God's help I'm going to leave my abusive marriage. Lord, help, me to plan wisely and protect me and my children until we are safely away from this abuse.*

⚜ WORDS FROM JEENIE ⚜

Debbie asked God to help her convince her husband that she was a good wife. Kenny dug in his heels and resisted big-time. He was unwilling to change.

All through Debbie's story, the control by Kenny is quite evident. No amount of asking, pleading, begging, or being good could change his mind. He felt no compulsion, as do many abusers, to give a valid reason. It was basically, "Because I said so." End of discussion.

Some become further enraged when they are drunk, and the verbal, physical, and emotional abuse can be enormous.

Debbie's question, "Can I please go to the church baptism and picnic?" reminds us of the childhood game called Mother, May I? All the kids stood on a straight horizontal line. The child who was "Mother" stood at the front facing them, and as each one asked, "Mother, may I?" she determined how large their step would be toward her. Usually she only allowed baby steps, when the children were hoping for giant steps. Mother was in control, and all the kids were at her beck and call—at her mercy.

In the marriage, Kenny had established his control. Debbie courageously decided to leave Kenny. It was an extremely brave and scary decision. However, she was certain God would get her through. And He did.

> *"Come to me, all you who are weary and burdened, and I will give you rest. Take my yoke upon you and learn from me, for I am gentle and humble in heart, and you will find rest for your souls. For my yoke is easy and my burden is light"* (Matthew 11:28–30).

Marigold helplessly watched her husband change, but since he was considered a pillar in the church, who would believe her?

NO ONE WOULD BELIEVE ME
MARIGOLD

My husband had ignored our 30th wedding anniversary. I tried not to dwell on how hurt I was. What on earth had happened to change Argyle so much?

The ringing of the phone broke into my thoughts as I walked down the hall. Stepping around the corner, I saw Argyle hold out the receiver. "Don Hooper," he said.

Don, one of the church ushers, was probably calling with a ministry question. I took the phone. "Hello," I started to say, but broke off at the dial tone in my ear. Feeling foolish, I rolled my eyes and hung up. Then I looked at my husband questioningly.

"Don wants you to call him back," Argyle said.

So he knew Don had already hung up! However, wanting to avoid an argument, I said nothing to Argyle and dutifully returned Don's call to supply the information he needed. Later that evening, with a continuing sense of duty, I sat near Argyle's recliner for our devotional time. Even though he'd been a church board member for years, Argyle had never been interested in reading the Bible and praying with me. Counselors assigned us, as homework, to have devotions together, hoping it would draw us closer.

Instead of opening the Bible, Argyle scowled. "The other day you accused me of rolling my eyes at you. Well, you rolled yours at me when Don called."

My stomach twisted. I had hoped for a peaceful evening, but maybe it still wasn't too late to avoid a land mine. The eye-rolling incident had happened when I'd suggested that we watch a movie together. I was still wounded at how my husband had reacted. Now I had to choose my words carefully.

Argyle stared at me, impatient for a response.

"Well," I began, "I felt rejected when you rolled your eyes at my suggestion. That's different from rolling my eyes at myself because I felt ridiculous talking to a dead phone line."

Argyle's response to such a statement was usually a long period of silence. Sometimes neither of us said anything for up to 40 minutes, usually depending on how long I could wait. If I gave up and tried to leave the room, he became angry. That was the pattern.

But this night he broke the pattern. "You are wrong!" he bellowed.

My jaw dropped. "You can't say my feelings are wrong!"

"You've said it to me."

"I have not!"

"Yes, you have," he insisted. "You've also said my feelings don't matter."

This crazy talk unnerved me. I had certainly never said Argyle's feelings didn't matter. Of course they mattered. What I'd done was try to point out that when he used the phrase "I feel," he wasn't revealing actual feelings, such as joy, sadness, anger, or disappointment. Instead, he stated assumptions: "I don't feel you want to spend time with me. I feel you don't care about me. I feel like you want me dead."

Appalled, I reassured him every time that his assumptions weren't based on fact.

"That's how I feel," he insisted. End of discussion.

Now, Argyle returned to the previous night's incident. "I never refused to watch the movie with you. You're the one who left the room."

Technically he was right. Whenever he didn't answer with words, I had only his sighs, grunts, and facial expressions to go by. But even without uttering a sound, he couldn't have been clearer about his disinterest in my motion picture suggestion.

I struggled not to cry. "If I was a stronger woman, and if I hadn't already been hurt at no anniversary present or card from you, maybe I could have dealt with the Don Hooper thing better."

Argyle shifted his gaze. "Sorry about that. But I didn't know what to get you, and you don't want me to spend no stinkin' money. I've been real busy anyway and didn't have time to get you anything."

But you do find time to spend hours at the coffee shop every afternoon, supposedly praying through your prayer list, I thought. *And you drop whatever you're doing to meet with anyone who asks for spiritual advice and counsel.*

At the onset of panic attacks ten years previously, Argyle had begun seeing a counselor. Not wanting to detract from our leadership roles, we told no one for a long time. Argyle was on the elder board, and I directed women's ministries at our church. Also, some of our friends and family didn't believe in professional counseling. They felt that problems were best resolved by spending more time "praying through at the altar" rather than using what they considered "worldly" methods such as psychotherapy.

I had ample reason to "pray through." Argyle had been withdrawing emotionally for a long time. Although he still made a point to say the words, "I love you," his extreme passivity toward me had changed over the years to deep disrespect and hostility.

I read dozens of counseling books to learn how to improve myself and our marriage. In response to the advice, I was open with him about what I preferred in our relationship. That attempt backfired. Whatever I liked eventually became what he refused to give me. I never dreamed that a man who once said he loved me would treat me that way.

If I tried to confront him about anything, he would snarl, "Meowww!" to indicate I was being catty. Fear that he would tell someone I was unsubmissive shut me down immediately. I couldn't face the prospect of losing the approval of others.

One book on verbal abuse described Argyle's behavior so accurately, I almost wondered if the author had been watching us on a hidden video-recording device. Often I wished I *could* have access to video evidence of what was actually said and done behind closed doors. I feared that without such backup, no one would believe me.

⮜ WORDS FROM JEENIE ⮞

Undoubtedly both Argyle and Marigold were respected and valued by the people in their church. I would not be surprised if many a wife told her husband while in a fight, "Why can't you be more like Argyle?" Little did they know what went on behind closed doors. People can fight all the way to church and upon arrival, put on the charm and create a false impression. This couple's positional status (elder and women's ministry director) worked to their advantage at church.

A controller and abuser will constantly look for and point out perceived inadequacies on the part of their mate. And, faults are easy to find, as we are all imperfect. But the constant criticisms and putdowns from an abuser weave a web of control, chipping away at the victim's self-esteem and diminishing her feelings of empowerment to leave the relationship.

Ignoring the 30th anniversary, as well as the counselor's advice of reading the Bible and praying together, was a way in which Argyle hurt and antagonized his wife.

Then, when the abuser acts in a loving way, he reminds the victim of why she fell for him in the first place. This causes confusion and uncertainty with the person suffering the abuse, and can be used as a control mechanism. Abuser: "I can be loving if you, the victim, comply with my demands." The abuser is placing the blame on the victim for the abuser's choice to abuse.

In the context of this relationship, when Argyle stated, "I do not feel like you want to spend time with me. I feel like you don't care about me. I feel like you want me dead," it was likely manipulation and an attempt to make Marigold feel guilty and responsible for his behavior.

HOPE BEYOND THE DARKNESS
CHARLES R. BROWN

In the darkness
there is fear and lostness—
hopelessness.
In the dumps there is the
putrid odor of rotting things—
things pushed around,
covered, buried—
fear and bruising and shame.
The weight of aloneness
unbearable.

The hole seems too deep,
the climb beyond your strength.
Darkness—
to the left, to the right,
inside, outside,
above and below.

Why, O God? Why?
At last, you have asked
in the right direction.

> *You, Lord, keep my lamp burning;*
> *my God turns my darkness into light.*
> —PSALM 18:28

There is hope beyond the darkness!

Sophia was fortunate to have a brother who was willing to act as her bodyguard, but how long could she keep depending on him? And how long would he be willing to stay at her house and protect her?

THE BODYGUARD
CARLO RODRIGUEZ

In fifth grade, I got my first job as a chaperone for my sister, Sophia, fulfilling the tradition of my Mexican ancestors. Thirty years later, my role matured, and I am now her bodyguard.

Three years ago, Sophia's husband ran off with his intern. The betrayal after 20 years of marriage deeply disturbed her. I encouraged her to take time to heal and to discern the type of man God might place in her life. But, instead, within a year, she found Abdul. He told her how angelic she looked and how he wanted to protect her from all harm. And so, what I perceived as the rebound romance began with gusto. Within weeks, he was living with her in a way God meant exclusively for a man and his wife.

She seemed happy, so my family welcomed Abdul, his mom, four sisters, and two brothers, as well as their culture of drums and violins, dancing, singing, and Moroccan traditions into our holidays and holy days. We made the tamales that are a part of our culture, they made the kabobs. They liked us. We liked them.

But within a few months, I noticed he doubted our acceptance of him, and he became obsessive over her free time. He'd ask her where she'd been and why she was with her sisters and not him. She seemed to like his jealousy—at first. It made her feel wanted. As more months went by, though, he didn't even want us to visit her.

Increasingly, she told me of incidents like this one: "Abdul pushed all the stuff off the counter—just because I walked away from him while he was talking to me. He broke two lamps and a gumball machine. Those gumballs went flying everywhere! I had to clean up the mess myself."

I asked her, "Why are you staying with him?"

"He has good moments," she replied. "Anyway, I told him I'd hurt him bad if he ever laid a hand on me."

I'm sure others saw how Abdul's aggression steadily progressed over time and almost seemed predictable My fears for her became a reality on a Friday night two months ago when I picked up her call.

"Carlo!" she yelled.

"What happened?" I asked after hearing a whack.

"Carlo! Ow! Help!"

The phone went dead, so I called the police. When I got to her house, the sergeant was handing her an ice pack to put on her bruised face.

I'll kill him, I thought.

"What happened?" I asked.

"We had a bad argument," she said. "I started to pick up the phone, and he told me not to. So when I called you, he hit me. The police got here really fast, but he ran off when he heard the sirens."

I told the sergeant we wanted to file charges, but she said no. The sergeant advised her to get a restraining order. Without one, the police could only respond to our calls, but they wouldn't be able to stop him from coming near her. But she said no to that too.

Instead she asked me, "Will you stay here tonight?"

I stayed for several nights, which made Abdul angry. I got numerous text messages from him saying I was taking his place and needed to leave, but I didn't leave. So he found other ways to get her attention. He came through the window while we were both at work and took her keys, passport, Social Security card, and even some jewelry. He also went through her emails and downloaded intimate videos of her and her ex-husband. Then he called Sophia to say she could have her belongings back if she would meet with him for five minutes.

I asked her, "If the black eye and the obsessive text messages aren't enough, is breaking and entering your home and burglary enough? Will you get a restraining order now?"

"I don't have time to go through all that hassle. And, anyway, it'll be really hard for him to get work if that's on his record."

"I know you want to protect him even after all this," I said, "but I can't be your bodyguard forever."

"Look, I don't want to make him angrier than he already is. I know he'll calm down with time."

"But he's in his car, watching the house all hours of the night, waiting for me to leave. He's not calming down," I said, utterly frustrated. So two months after the first police call, I'm still sleeping on her couch. And after reading up to 50 text messages every day to me and to her, I'm scared of what he's really capable of. I stop on one message I hadn't noticed before and think about it: "The honeymoon is over."

"Why did you stay with him?" I asked her again today.

She thought for a moment and said, "I guess I loved his family more than him. If I could marry them, I would."

"I know. They're a lot of fun, but here's the deal," I said. "Rebounding with Abdul, living with his abuse, and still protecting him affects my life as much as yours. I love you, sis, but you have to make wiser decisions from now on. Wisdom comes from God, so ask Him for it. And get the restraining order. Otherwise, I'm going back to my own home."

I'm giving her a few days to make this decision. In the meantime, I'm scrolling through hundreds of texts to note the ones that will prove to a judge he's psycho. They all seem to work.

⤳ WORDS FROM JEENIE ⤶

Stalking and harassing is abuse. Victims of abuse can have twisted thoughts and behaviors. Sometimes victims recant their stories for a variety of reasons, namely fear of repercussions, and in response to threats from the abuser. In my practice, I have seen many abusers do bizarre things, almost without limits, in order to be in control once again. Sadly, at times it works and the victim acquiesces.

But abuse is abuse and cannot be tolerated.

REFLECTION: Has your marriage turned out differently than you first imagined? Do you feel betrayed?

PRAYER: *Lord, love means to care, honor means to respect, and cherish means to adore. Isn't that true? Lord, I feel so alone. In Jesus' name I pray, amen.*

"My husband was a respected surgeon, yet our family lived in fear of him. His treatment of us was inhumane and we felt hopeless. After 20 years of marriage, I was able to break away and begin a new life for us."

—SALLY

CHAPTER 4

Prisoner of Fear

The Lord is my light and my salvation—
whom shall I fear?
The Lord is the stronghold of my life—
of whom shall I be afraid?
—PSALM 27:1

IN DANGEROUS SITUATIONS our brains sound an alarm, kicking in what is known as the fight-or-flight response. With rapid heartbeats, sweaty hands, and shallow breaths we are ready to defend ourselves or make a quick getaway. Most of us have experienced a fearful situation and understand how quickly our bodies react to red flags that signal impending danger.

One evening Karen picked up a takeout order of pizza and headed to her car. Just as she inserted her key in the car door, a threatening voice behind her yelled, "Get in the van, lady!"

Glancing over her shoulder, she saw two scruffy-looking men standing by a blue van. She yelled back, "No way!" By her quick response she gained the attention of several people walking by. Then she quickly opened her car door, jumped in, and locked the doors. As she drove out of the parking lot, she looked in her rearview mirror and saw the blue van heading in the opposite direction. Karen is grateful she responded quickly to the red flag situation.

However, if the person behind your fear is not a stranger, but someone you're married to or dating, reactions to red flags become more difficult. The voice once so endearing has turned cruel, the eyes once so promising now reflect hate. The touch once so comforting has turned painful. Broken promises from the abuser become a cycle of betrayal. The ability to reason rationally is impaired and fear increases. Minds swirl with unanswered questions: *What can I do? Where can I go? Who's going to believe me?*

When abuse accelerates, fear of the abuser becomes a shadow that follows the victim—to school events, dental appointments, grocery shopping, and even church. You cancel a doctor's appointment because you don't want your doctor to ask about the bruises on your body. Fear whispers, *Leave.* Moments later, another voice whispers, *He'll make you suffer if you leave.* The tug-of-war continues, and fear forms a prison.

A domestic abuse victim's fear of the abuser is justified, particularly when she considers leaving the relationship because that is the most dangerous time for the victim. Women have been severely injured and even killed when attempting to leave the relationship, which is why safety planning and supportive services are critical to safely escaping an abusive relationship.

The following stories demonstrate how others found hope through God and were set free of fear.

Fearful for her life and the lives of her precious twins, Judi got the courage to run away from her abusive husband one Sunday morning. God led her to a warm, loving church, and this is her story.

JUDI'S STORY
SHARYN MCDONALD

I noticed her the moment she walked through the door—painfully thin, wearing ragged jeans and a white T-shirt. Her two adorable preschoolers clung to her like a life preserver. She seemed nervous and ill at ease as her eyes darted around the small sanctuary. She found a place to sit in the corner of the back row and placed a child on either side of her.

I walked to the back of the sanctuary and sat down beside her. "Hi, my name is Sharyn. I don't believe I've seen you here before."

She smiled weakly and replied, "My name is Judi. I haven't been here before. I really don't know why I came."

Just then the service began, and our conversation temporarily ended. At times Judi wept and held her children close. Sometimes she seemed distracted, and at other times she seemed to listen with rapt attention.

Her pain cried out to my heart, and after the service, I invited her to lunch. While the children played, she slowly began to share her story.

"I was 17 when I met my husband. He was 24, good-looking, and had a hot car. My parents did not like him and tried to break us up, but we eloped anyway. After we married, my husband told me he loved me too much to share me with anyone and didn't want our families interfering with our marriage. We cut all ties with my parents, family, and friends. It was sad for me, but it all seemed so romantic—just the two of us together, not needing anyone or anything but each other."

She paused for a moment, tears filling her eyes. "I never saw the warning signs. After we were married for six months I got pregnant, and the honeymoon was over."

At first, her husband used words as his weapon of choice. "He started telling me I was stupid, ugly, and worthless. He taunted me in front of his friends. Then the pushing, shoving, and punching began. When he hit me in the stomach, I was terrified of losing the babies. Thankfully, although they made their debut a little early, both twins were beautiful and healthy."

I smiled and said, "Yes, your children are beautiful."

Although Judi was the focus of his anger and violent behavior, having two babies in the house was stressful. Sadly, the cycle of violence and abuse, followed by emotional pleas for forgiveness, continued. At one point, her pleas for him to stop beating her seemed to reach him, and she began to be hopeful.

"Then one day he started screaming at me again and calling me names. He pushed me down the steps, breaking my leg. I grew more concerned about my children's safety and my own. I should have left him then, but I was afraid and didn't know where to go. My friends and family were no longer part of my life, and I was alone—and ashamed."

The abuse continued, and Judi grew even more fearful for herself and her children. "One day out of desperation I left while he was at work, but he found me. He drug me home and beat me severely, breaking my nose. As I lay there bleeding, he took a gun and pointed it at my head. He screamed and cursed at me and told me if I ever left again he would kill me, but he would kill the twins first and make me watch before he let me die."

Judi was terrified of staying with him and more terrified of leaving, but eventually had, with great courage. That Sunday morning was the first day she had been on her own. Going to church that morning, sharing her story with a stranger, and seeking refuge was an act of courage. She found more than a compassionate listening ear that day; she found hope.

For the next several weeks her family was moved from one church family to another until we could find a more permanent home for them. Each family who offered shelter to Judi and the twins was warned that housing them might put their own safety, and in some cases that of their children, at risk. The danger was real, based on her husband's violent and abusive nature and the fact that he was obsessed with finding her. Even knowing the risk, they opened their hearts and homes to her.

Her new faith in Christ gave her both strength and hope. For safety purposes she changed her name, and within a month she relocated to a shelter in another state where she found the safety, encouragement, and love she longed for.

WORDS FROM JEENIE

Judi thought she had finally found a safe haven when she discovered the man who promised to protect, love, and care for her—forever. She fell into the arms of a man whom she believed would bring wholeness and happiness, not realizing her husband was weaving a web of deceit, manipulation, and control. Then it hit the fan.

Cutting off people in her life, she was alone with no one available to talk to, or to reveal what was happening in her life. She undoubtedly felt forsaken and abandoned—exactly what her husband had planned, a common tactic for control, in order to begin the cycle of abuse.

Abuse seemed to come from nowhere—out of the blue. She didn't see it coming and she did not go looking for abuse. It just erupted. As is typical after the first stages of physical abuse, Judi's husband was sorrowful, repentant, and pleaded for another chance. In tears he promised it would never happen again. Things looked up and were good for a time—the honeymoon period. But, honeymoons always come to an end. Not too long afterwards, abuse became a common occurrence, and one without apologies or regrets.

Various studies indicate that domestic violence often accelerates during pregnancy. In an Association of Women's

Health, Obstetrics, and Neonatal Nursing study, "Why Batter-ing During Pregnancy?" respondents shared their thoughts. When asked why they *thought* they were abused during their pregnancies, answers categorize into four contexts:
- Jealousy toward the unborn child
- Anger towards the unborn child
- Pregnancy specific violence not directed toward the child
- "Business as usual."

What a brave young woman Judi was to grab her toddlers and flee. Women's shelters confirm that thousands of women remain in horrific abuse because of the threat of death from their husbands.

Judi found help at a church from a stranger who took time to listen and care. What a wonderful, ministering church that protected and housed Judi and her little ones for a time.

Judi made a wise choice to change her name and move to another state to begin life anew, far away from the abuse she had suffered. It took amazing courage.

Diane experienced one of the worst nightmares a mother can have when her son failed to pick her up at the airport.

ARMED AND DANGEROUS
DIANE GARDNER

I sat on the bench outside the baggage claim area at Ontario International Airport and shivered from the cool, damp October air. I glanced at my watch—9:30 P.M.—over an hour since my son Curtis was due to pick me up. I called his beeper again with no response.

A man walked over to me and asked, "Are you Diane Gardner?" When I nodded, he said, "I'm Detective Smith." He flashed his badge and took a driver's license from his pocket. "Do you know this man?" he asked.

I felt uneasy. No one gives up their driver's license to anyone. Was there a car accident involving this man and Curtis? Does the detective think I know something?

I answered, "No, I don't recognize him."

"Do you drive a red Cadillac license number . . . ?" he continued.

I was shocked. Why did he ask me about my car? Oh no! Was Curtis in a terrible wreck? I took a deep breath, "Yes, I do."

The detective showed me two other pictures. He asked, "Is this your son Curtis and is this his ex-wife, Karen?"

I responded with a surprised tone of voice, "Yes, that is my son and my daughter-in-law."

He looked intently into my eyes and said, "Well, Ms. Gardner, I'm sorry to tell you this. Warren, the man whose license I have, was shot in the head at close range today. We think he's your ex-daughter-in-law's boyfriend. He's in the hospital having surgery and is in critical condition. This took place outside Karen's apartment in Corona around 1:00 P.M. Curtis allegedly shot him, kidnapped his ex-wife, and drove off in a red Cadillac. A neighbor gave us the license number. DMV shows the car is registered to you. Three children were abandoned at the scene and taken in by a neighbor. The children told the police it was their daddy who shot Warren and took their mommy with him. Mr. Warren's son is with his grandparents, and your grandchildren are with Karen's parents."

I felt as if time and my heart had both stopped. I jumped up and stumbled to the edge of the curb. I looked up and yelled, "No! No! Jesus!" I felt filled with dismay and disbelief. I thought, *How could this happen?*

I swallowed the lump in my throat and asked, "How'd you

know I was here and that Curtis was supposed to pick me up?"

"We found Curtis's brother in Riverside and brought him in for questioning. Carlton wanted to leave because he said Curtis was scheduled to pick you up at the airport. We told him he had to stay at the station, and we would take care of you."

After giving my statement at the police station, Detective Jay, who was a friend from church, went back with Carlton and me to my house. Every few minutes there was a news report with my son's picture and the description of my car. Every reporter sounded as if they were shouting at me. "Armed and dangerous! Armed and dangerous! This suspect is armed and dangerous!"

I knew he was armed. I could never minimize that horrible fact, but I hated hearing those words over and over like he was on a shooting rampage. I felt sick to my stomach to know my child, who knew the Lord, allowed his mind to become so darkened by the enemy that he would deliberately seriously hurt other people. Curtis had given in completely to the temptation to do evil. He ignored all the warnings from his heavenly Father. James 1:13–14 says:

When tempted, no one should say, "God is tempting me." For God cannot be tempted by evil, nor does he tempt anyone; but each person is tempted when they are dragged away by their own evil desire and enticed.

At 2:00 A.M. Detective Jay received a call. He took me aside from everyone. "The police received a call from a security patrol. He saw a car fitting the description of your car parked at the abandoned military houses across the street from our church. I need to go." He paused and looked compassionately at me. "I'll call you as soon as I can." Then he left.

As Jay headed toward the helicopter light that hovered over my abandoned car, he heard screams coming from the darkness. He stopped his car, rolled his window down, and put his hand on his gun. In the moonlight, he saw Karen run from behind the school next door to our church. She was screaming hysterically. With gun drawn, he called her name.

She could tell it was Detective Jay, someone she knew. "Jay, thank you, thank you," she said through her sobs.

"Where's Curtis?" he asked.

"He's gone! He told me to stay behind the school until he left if I wanted to live."

"We have law enforcement patrolling the area to look for Curtis. Don't worry." Jay grabbed a stack of napkins to apply pressure to Karen's bleeding hand. "I'll stay with you until the ambulance arrives."

She said through her sobs, "Jay, he beat me. I've never seen him like that. Curtis went crazy, yelling and screaming at me for hours about our divorce. Then he yelled some of the same things we saw in a movie last year where the guy shot the girl in the hand. Then Curtis shot me in the hand he said I used to sign the divorce papers. He was evil."

"I'm sorry he did that. We'll have you in the emergency room soon." Jay continued, "Karen, I'm here because they spotted his mom's car."

Karen anxiously asked, "Jay, where are my kids? He left the kids and Warren's son standing on the sidewalk next to Warren, crying. I asked him not to leave them, but he said someone will call the police, and they will take them in. Where are they?"

Jay said, "They're safe. They're with your parents. Warren's son is with his parents."

Karen sighed in relief and asked, "Where is my boyfriend, Warren? I know he was hurt bad."

"He's in surgery at the hospital," replied Detective Jay.

I wondered what to say to Warren's parents. I know they love their son as much as I love mine. What could the family of the violator say to the family of the victim? "I'm sorry my family hurt your family"? I sent a bouquet of flowers to the hospital with a note that read how sorry I was that this happened. I don't know if they received the flowers or refused to accept them. What do you do when you are the parent of the perpetrator? There's a depth of sorrow we feel for the victims, but where is our legitimate outlet?

It was seven months before Curtis was apprehended and sent to prison. And it was two years before I was allowed to see my grandchildren again, but today we have a wonderful relationship. Jesus' grace has been enough to sustain me through all that has happened. As a result, I have been able to help others even while in the midst of my own trials.

～ WORDS FROM JEENIE ～

In an unhealthy relationship, the end of the relationship can be a very dangerous time for the person who decides to leave. Desperate people call for desperate measures.

Watch the news. It plays out a scenario of a distraught and furious husband over the impending separation or divorce, and it is not too uncommon for him to kill the lover, his wife, and himself. I've heard men say, "If I can't have her, no one can." Thus, the dastardly deed is executed. Seldom does he consider the pain it will cause his orphaned children, parents, or extended family.

Lieutenant Tom Tarpley, Special Operations Division commander, Tustin Police Department, California, has provided this information on how to be aware of the abuser.

DETECTIVE TOM'S TIP:
LAW ENFORCEMENT PROFILE OF AN ABUSER:

Look at the person's entire life. Look at the police reports: see if there is a pattern, if lots were generated, where he lived, if he often moved around. Obtain reports from agencies in various cities where he lived. Then look at the person himself. Does he lose his temper once in a while? Does he resort to physical violence? (1) With hands or (2) weapons. Law enforcement has a scale: verbal abuse to physical abuse to use of weapons. It's a significant concern if weapons were used. Abusers usually start with demeaning words, making the person feel small and weak, but some start directly with physical violence. If hands-on force doesn't get the desired results, a small amount of the population resort to stabbing, shooting, or hitting with a sharp object.

Abusers don't change for the better as they get older. They just become more abusive. Over and over again, I have seen abusers go to trial, go to jail, get out, and begin abuse all over again—either with the same woman or a different one. In one case, a man was on trial for murdering his girlfriend. Seven past girlfriends were brought in and testified against him.

Perpetrators' brains are wired to abuse. It is part of their DNA. It is all they know to do!

This story is written in memory of Kori and in hopes that other women who find themselves in a domestic violence situation will get out safely—and not go back.

A FATEFUL DECISION
SUSAN TITUS OSBORN

The phone rang late one evening, a call from my husband's brother-in-law, Elmer. "We've had a terrible tragedy in the family, and we want you to pray for Judy and me."

"What happened?" asked Dick.

"Our daughter Kori was murdered by her boyfriend last night. She was in an abusive relationship and had gotten a restraining order against Dennis a couple of weeks ago. She moved in with a girlfriend, but we talked her into coming home to South Dakota last week."

Elmer paused to regain his composure and then continued. "She packed her bag, bought a bus ticket, and was scheduled to come home day before yesterday. However, when she got to the bus depot, she was told her luggage was 7 pounds over the 50-pound allowance. Kori didn't have the money to pay the $40 overweight fee, so she decided to stay in Vancouver with her girlfriend one more night. We would've paid the fee, if only we'd known. She made the fatal mistake that night of going back to Dennis's house to get a few more personal items."

Dick knew Elmer wasn't up to telling him the details, so he said, "Let us know what we can do to help. Susan and I are here for you and Judy."

By reading newspaper articles, we were able to piece together the events of that tragic night. Apparently when Kori went back to Dennis's house to retrieve her personal belongings, he became enraged since she had left him. He apparently stabbed her, dragged her body across the yard into his car, and dumped her down a steep embankment nearby.

What began as a routine traffic stop in the early hours of the next morning turned into so much more. When the police pulled over Dennis's pickup for speeding, one officer noticed that the driver's hands, clothing, and face were covered in fresh blood.

Dennis claimed that he had just taken his severely injured black Labrador retriever to a veterinarian; but when the police checked the nearby veterinary hospitals, they found none had treated such a dog.

The situation looked suspicious from the beginning, so the police obtained a search warrant and went to Dennis's rental home. They discovered a pool of blood in the driveway and marks indicating something heavy was dragged from the house. They also found a broken knife blade in the living room and bloody knives in the kitchen sink.

Shortly after daylight, they found Kori's body about a half mile from where they stopped the pickup. She had been stabbed repeatedly. They immediately booked Dennis for murder.

The next time Dick talked to Judy, she cried and said between sobs, "I want to bring my baby home and bury her here, but I don't know how we're going to pay for it."

Dick replied, "Let us take care of that."

He called Kori's sister, Tammi, who lived in Vancouver. He got the information for the mortuary and called to arrange to have Kori's body shipped home to South Dakota. He also sent Tammi money for airfare so she could go home for the funeral.

Tammi said, "Kori's four-month relationship with Dennis started smoothly. He gave her roses and a new kitten, but it quickly became turbulent. During the incident two weeks ago that resulted in her obtaining the restraining order, he pulled out a chunk of her hair when she tried to call 911. I begged and pleaded with my sister to get away from him, and she was in the process. She was doing the right thing by moving on with her life. If only she would've left the overweight luggage and boarded the bus, she would be alive and on her way home to South Dakota."

❦ WORDS FROM JEENIE ❦

What a horrific and painful story. It brought tears, as I'm sure it did for everyone reading about the incident. Unless we have experienced a violent death of a child, we cannot fully understand or empathize.

Dennis depicts a controlling, manipulating, and abusive man. Often, if they can't have their girlfriend/wife, no one can. This opens the door wide to whatever destructive and violent behavior they muster up.

Kori was trying to free herself from Dennis and even got a restraining order. Likely when she tried to call 911, she realized her need to get away from Dennis—forever. Even with a legal document, a restraining order, victims of abuse may not be safe. Many abusers make choices with no regard for the law.

Dennis was a typical suitor, bearing gifts of roses and a kitten. An abuser, however, can quickly move from the most gregarious, outgoing, and loving suitor in the world to inflicting unspeakable violence in an instant.

God evidently led the police to stop Dennis on the traffic violation, follow the signs, and check his home while the evidence was still intact.

I'm sure Dick's offer to bring Kori home for burial and provide an airplane ticket to Tammi to attend the funeral brought a measure of comfort to a distraught family.

For many years, I have made it a practice to pray each morning for a family who is in the grieving process. I pray daily for one year, then write a note stating I have held them up to the Lord each day during their first year of mourning. Scripture states we need to: *Carry each other's burdens, and in this way you will fulfill the law of Christ* (Galatians 6:2).

REFLECTION: Has fear become your prison? What should you do to escape from the situation?

PRAYER: *Lord, every moment I am fearful. Deliver me from the fears that dominate me. Help me to believe that under Your wings I'll find safety. In Jesus' name we pray, amen.*

CHAPTER 5

The Effects of Abuse on Children and Teens

Fathers, do not provoke your children to anger by the way you treat them. Rather, bring them up with the discipline and instruction that comes from the Lord.
—Ephesians 6:4 (NLT)

A CHILD'S HEART and mind are imprinted for a lifetime by our actions and examples as parents. When domestic abuse erodes a child's safety and security, their self-esteem is damaged. Instead of feeling love, they feel anger and confusion. Instead of being hopeful, they become discouraged. Instead of trusting, they are wary. As they become teenagers—without appropriate intervention and support— corrosion of their hearts and minds may leave them vulnerable to harmful behaviors like the use of drugs or alcohol. In cases, the cycle of abuse continues.

The effects of abuse blow like an unrelenting wind, knocking down self-esteem, as wave upon wave of threats and violence drown a family in hopelessness. The aftermath can last a lifetime, causing poor choices, depression, anxiety, and suicidal thoughts or actions. But there is hope and help.

As Diane experienced, sometimes the signs of abuse are hard for a mother to see, especially when the child didn't know how to vocalize and the husband has a stellar reputation in the community.

MOVING ON

DIANE WILLIAMS

Katelyn was eight years old when it happened, but I remember it as though it were yesterday. I dropped her at her friend Megan's house to play while I attended a board meeting for a local residential facility that housed neglected, runaway, and abused teens. Mike, Katelyn's stepfather, was scheduled to pick her up and get her to bed while I was away.

Arriving home that night after the meeting, the house was quiet. Mike was at work on his laptop, as always. Everything appeared normal, so I said good night and went upstairs to bed.

The next morning after taking Katelyn to school, however, I received a phone call that changed the course of my marriage and parenting. It wasn't unusual for me to deal with frequent discord between Katelyn and Mike. I assumed that was normal for stepfamilies and tried to keep peace. Usually I'd even take Mike's side because I felt, as an adult, he must be telling the truth, while my young daughter was probably exaggerating to gain sympathy.

The concerned words of Megan's mother told me differently. When I answered the phone she said, "Diane, I don't know what's going on in your home, but I have never seen a child so terrified to get in a car with someone before. I almost didn't let her go. I just thought you'd want to know."

I thanked her and hung up the phone, stunned. It seemed my heart stopped beating for a moment as I recalled the many times I overlooked Katelyn's frustration with Mike, thinking she was overreacting.

Before tucking my daughter into bed that night, I asked her about the previous night. 'Why were you afraid to get in the car with Mike?"

She looked at me with that "doe in the headlights" look. I continued to press. "Did he do something to you? I really want to know."

Katelyn replied, "He tickles me too hard. It hurts."

I felt there was more to the story than that, but I had pushed Katelyn as far as I dared. Something inside told me it wasn't worth asking Mike about. But I vowed that day to never leave Katelyn alone with Mike again, not for one minute. And I kept that vow.

When Katelyn was 15, she and I prayed and researched for months before deciding to send her to a boarding school in Tennessee, although we lived in Kentucky. I spent two weekends with her every month until the end of that school year, and it was one of the best years of my daughter's teenage life. Often, within hours of my return, Mike's anger would spew at me in critical, rejecting words, but Katelyn's safety was foremost in my mind.

When Katelyn turned 16 and decided to come home, I made sure she had a car to drive, albeit an old one, so she could escape to a friend's house if she ever felt unsafe. I home-schooled her that year, and she completed her junior and senior education requirements in one school year. Graduating at 17, she chose a college in Florida; but by the second year, she was lost in the wrong crowd, while her grades plummeted and her drinking increased.

Today at 23, Katelyn struggles with emotional eating, weight problems, a lack of self-esteem, and anger. Her emotional challenges are evident in all of her relationships. She has a difficult time relaxing and trusting people in general. I understand why, although I was never able to find out the extent of Mike's emotional abuse toward her.

Mike is a leader in the local and national Christian community, and he knows how to "talk the talk." His problem is with his "walk."

Three months ago, Katelyn made a decision not to see Mike for a while, maybe never again. She said she needs to just "be herself" without his criticism and control dominating her daily life. We talked about her decision for weeks, and I strongly encouraged her to do what was best for her as a single mom and for her two-year-old son, Jason.

Despite knowing Mike would be angry because he wouldn't get to see our grandson anymore, I held firm and told Katelyn, "I support your decision. You're doing the right thing." And I believe with all my heart that she is.

It's only been 90 days, but I already see the positive changes in her life. The increase in Katelyn's self-esteem, her 25-pound weight loss, and the joy I'm beginning to witness in her daily attitude and behavior confirm the benefits of her distancing herself from Mike.

She still struggles, but she now recognizes that her step-father's anger was not her fault. It was never *her* fault. Mike is a broken man who refuses to get help. Katelyn's job now is to focus on healing, on loving and raising Jason, and working toward the goals and dreams God has placed on her heart.

God is good. He led Katelyn to set firm boundaries to protect her heart and mind from further emotional and psychological abuse. I, too, have made some difficult decisions in the past few months. I obtained a legal separation from Mike and moved out of our marital dream house to a cozy 100-year-old rental where I am finally enjoying a peaceful existence and where I, too, can begin to heal.

My daughter and I are trusting God to lead us one day at a time to a place of peace, love, laughter, and joy.

～ WORDS FROM JEENIE ～

Children have tender hearts. A look can crush their emotions. Angry words—blaming, accusing, and degrading—can cause great damage. Even birth fathers often go too far with a child.

As a therapist, I wonder about the statement Katelyn made at eight years of age: "He tickles me too hard." I strongly suspect that is the only way she could describe sexual abuse. Now, as an adult and mother of Jason, Katelyn suffers from emotional issues, weight problems, lack of self-esteem, and anger, which brings me to the conclusion it may have been more than verbal and emotional abuse. Tickling can be a sign. While difficult to prove sexual abuse, a parent might be concerned. Parents who are concerned should seek professional help. Abuse suffered as a child can have a lifelong impact, and professional counseling is often necessary to help adults cope and begin to heal from the abuse inflicted on them as a child.

As most parents do, Katelyn's mom did what she felt was within her control to protect her daughter, even if it meant being separated from her child. Parents make difficult decisions seeking to protect their kids.

Diane stated Mike was looked at as exemplary in the local and national Christian community, a position that he strove to keep in place. He evidently wished to look like a religious, devout, and family man. Yet, as was stated, he did not "walk the walk."

Abusers are manipulative, and most do not look like monsters. In fact, quite the opposite is true. Abusers who are in positions of prestige and authority within the community are often the last people we suspect, yet time and again we are proven wrong as their stellar reputations are used as a tool to silence their victims. When the community perceives the abuser to be a model citizen, this often makes it more confusing for the child victim and more dangerous for her to reveal his secret.

I've counseled numerous "godly" men in therapy who looked good in the Christian and secular world—ones who abused their families in various degrees. All is not as it appears. It is good that both Katelyn and her mother have moved away from Mike and are leading more emotionally healthy lives. I applaud their bravery.

What started out as a nice family outing in the mountains turned deadly and became the scariest day of young Margie's life.

THE SCARIEST DAY
MARGIE RAY

Every Saturday Mom packed a picnic lunch and our family went up in the mountains for the day. Our family included Mom, Andrew (11), Joe (8), me (7), and Crow who was Mom's seventh husband. At first glance, we looked like the typical family, laughing and enjoying an outing together. But as the day wore on, more relatives arrived and everyone started drinking.

One particular Saturday stands out in my mind as one of the scariest days of my life. The adults had been drinking for a couple of hours, and Crow lay down on a blanket and went to sleep.

Mom heard the boys giggling and knew they were up to something. She warned, "Don't mess with his boots and keys. He'll really be mad."

Crow had taken off his boots and laid his wallet and keys next to them. Joe grabbed his keys, stuffed them in one of Crow's boots, and moved it a couple of feet away. Andrew followed his brother's example and grabbed the other boot, put the wallet in it, and moved it. At the time these seemed like harmless pranks.

When Crow woke up, he didn't see his boots at first. He always had to be in charge, and he was furious. When he looked at Mom, she was sitting on a rock nearby and laughing, which made him even angrier. He picked up a rock as big as a baseball and hurled it at her. He hit her in the middle of her forehead, and she fell over on the ground.

When I heard a loud thump, I turned around and saw Mom lying there in a fetal position. She wasn't moving, and I thought she was dead. I looked at Crow and screamed, "You killed Mom!"

My brothers were both screaming too, and I thought Crow was going to kill us all. I ran up the hill as fast as my legs would carry me and started running down the highway, sobbing every step of the way.

Crow walked over to Mom, dragged her to the car, and tossed her into the passenger seat. She was still unconscious. He looked at the boys and said, "You better get in the car if you don't want me to kill her right here."

The boys solemnly complied. Crow drove the car beside me on the highway and shouted, "If you don't get in the car this instant, I'm going to kill you."

I immediately climbed in the car. I looked at Mom, and she started moaning. Then I realized she wasn't dead.

Crow took her to the hospital and then drove us home where our grandparents waited for us. No one said a word about the incident. A couple of hours later, Crow brought Mom home with her head swathed in a bandage and blood all over her shirt. Then Mom and Crow started joking around with each other as if nothing had happened.

Fortunately, Crow only spent weekends with us. He worked at a meatpacking plant about an hour and a half away, so he said he had an apartment near his work. Eventually we found out that was a lie. He was actually married to another woman and had children by her. He spent the weekdays with her and the weekends with us. I never did find out how he explained to her that he was gone every weekend. Nor did I know why Mom tolerated this arrangement after she found out.

On Saturday nights, there was often a party at our house. The guests brought their guns, and when they began drinking, they began shooting. I always hid in my closet and prayed. My grandparents took us to church every Sunday, so I learned to depend on Jesus as my Savior at a young age. I always felt I had the Holy Spirit inside me, and no matter how scary the circumstances, He would protect me.

Often we kids were shuffled around, staying with grandparents for a month, and then an aunt and uncle for a couple of weeks, then on to another family. We were rarely home for more than a few days at a time. My favorite place to stay, though, was at our next-door neighbors' house. They had a little girl my age.

Eventually the neighbors got fed up with the shooting and drinking. They thought we kids were in danger, so they called social services. Joe, now 10, moved in with our grandparents, and Andrew, now 13, stayed with Mom. The neighbors tried to adopt me, but Mom would not cooperate, so at age 9, I went to live with Catholic sisters. For the first time I felt safe, and I could concentrate on my studies.

As an adult, I learned Mom was bipolar and schizophrenic and seldom took her medicine. When she was dying, I went to visit her. I felt no bitterness or anger. I lay my head on her chest, and she took her hand and rubbed my hair. She was showing me she was sorry, and it gave me closure.

Marriage was easy for me. I so desperately wanted to have a normal, happy family. Today I am blessed with an incredible husband, two wonderful sons, and two beautiful grandchildren, whom I adore. And when difficulties in life arise, I sit in my favorite chair (my new closet) and pray.

ᘛ WORDS FROM JEENIE ᘙ

Here is another tragic and terrifying story of a manipulator and controller. Crow was as dishonest as they come. Actually, a polygamist. His skill was evident in his amazing ability to convince two wives and children that he was an upstanding man. The danger he inflicted on this family is almost unimaginable.

Yet it is a story of hope, as Margie describes her life of faith and her own family that she nurtured, and as evidenced in her ability to forgive.

Margie's hope was in Christ, established through the loving and spiritual training of her grandparents. She also found a place of safety cloistered with Catholic nuns who were nurturing, understanding, and watchful. It reminds us that all things are possible with God, who can turn tragedy into triumph, no matter the sufferings inflicted upon us.

DETECTIVE TOM'S TIP:
LIFE-ALTERING EFFECTS ON CHILDREN:

Children are present in 60 to 70 percent of all domestic violence situations. The other 30 to 40 percent represents dating relationships, where no kids are involved, because they haven't had kids yet. I see kids, ages 9 to 10, who witnessed domestic violence in the home; then at ages 20 to 30, they are arrested for their own violent crimes. They have kids, and the cycle continues. Generations of doom: the victims become the perpetrators. Kids who are exposed to violence often become violent. Although that it is not always the case, the police often deal with the same people over and over, and their kids are being set up for failure.

Diane had a nightmare that occurred over and over for ten years. It left her scared and shaken.

THE RECURRING NIGHTMARE
DIANE GARDNER

A recurring nightmare haunted me from ages 5 to 15. My parents were arguing so loudly I woke up and went to see what was wrong. I entered the living room in time to see Dad pick up the heavy black telephone and hit Mom in the head with it. Blood squirted like a faucet. I let out a loud scream.

Dad snatched my arm and shouted, "Shut up! What's wrong with you?"

"I'm . . . scared."

Dad let go of my arm, and Mom grabbed the other arm and said, "Let's go!"

We got in the car, and Mom drove to the hospital to get stitches. She held a bloody towel to her head with one hand and drove with the other. I stared at her and the bloody towel in silence. I had never seen so much blood. The nightmare always ended as we entered the hospital doors.

Each time I awakened from this nightmare, I was shaking. I told myself, "Stop shaking. It's only a dream. Mom and Dad argue a lot, but they never hit each other."

One day while I was combing Mom's hair when I was 15, I noticed an indentation on Mom's forehead just below her hairline. "Mom, how did you get this dent in your skull? Were you a little girl when it happened?"

Mom said sharply, "You know what happened. You were there and saw everything."

Unfortunately, I didn't have a clue what experience she referred to. To get her talking about the incident I said, "Oh yeah. How old was I when that happened?"

"You were 5. That was the night Dad hit me in the head with the telephone. You came in the room so I took you and drove myself to the hospital for stitches. Surely you remember that."

"I do . . . re . . . member," I said slowly. Oh no, that recurring nightmare was—real. My subconscious mind took that traumatic incident and buried it so deep that it only surfaced as a dream. For ten years I didn't realize this was an actual event that had happened. I had no idea why I kept having that recurring nightmare. Yet once I learned the truth, the nightmares ended.

After this incident my parents must have made an agreement to end physical violence in front of their kids since my siblings and I don't recall any physical altercations after that. However, they continued to argue constantly, and I was always afraid one of them would leave. My parents never did divorce, though, and neither one of them ever left.

The constant tension in our house caused me to become fearful. As a teenager, I was always trying to fix things—trying to find ways to make my parents love each other. But my efforts were to no avail. Our parents provided for us children and showed us love, but they only seemed to tolerate each other.

As an adult, I still find myself trying to fix people. However, the Lord has helped me use this for His glory, and I am no longer fearful. I've ministered to and encouraged women for more than 30 years and am a frequent speaker at women's conferences. As a pastor, I have counseled numerous couples and abuse victims. I've seen victims take hold of the Lord and His Word as well as violators turn their lives around and grow once again in the Lord. However, it's a journey, although never quick, that can result in success.

~✢ WORDS FROM JEENIE ✢~

Our conscious/unconscious is like a triangle. The small portion at the top represents the conscious level in which we live and the much larger bottom of the triangle contains the unconscious. I've done quite a bit of dream therapy with clients over the years, and each time a vivid dream is related to me, I lift up a prayer for God's wisdom and guidance.

The unconscious level is buried deeply within us, and sometimes it will surface in our dreams. Generally it consists of feelings and thoughts that we may find difficult to process in the light of day. Therefore, we unknowingly pushed them downward. Such was the case with Diane. The reality was too shocking for a child to absorb or deal with, so she buried it. However it was resurrected in her dreams. It would not surprise me if it also emerged when she heard her parents fighting in the night.

In therapy, I've warned many fighting couples that even behind closed doors, children are aware and frightened. They are always waiting for something terrible to happen—a divorce, brutality, etc. Even if it doesn't, as was the case in this story, the child is still tormented and terrified. Preverbal children and babies, whom the parents thought were sleeping soundly, can also be affected and unable to communicate their fears.

Once the nightmares were brought into the conscious level, Diane was able to deal rationally and move on.

Though we cannot always control what happens to us in life, we can control our responses to it, as did Diane. She was able to face the truth, accept it, and reach out to others in need.

Susan reached out to a troubled student by believing and encouraging her. Only God knows how a moment of kindness can change the outcome in someone else's life.

THE ESSAY
SUSAN TITUS OSBORN

Chills ran down my spine as I read Shelley's essay for the fiction writing class I was teaching at a local Christian college. *This seems so real,* I thought. *I don't think she could make this up.*

After rereading the essay and praying about it, I wrote a note at the bottom of Shelley's paper: If this story is true, please see me after class.

That evening I handed out the essays to the 20 students in my class at the end of my lecture. I said, "You did a nice job on your stories. Please follow my suggestions, and turn in another draft next week. At the end of the semester, be prepared to read your story aloud. You are dismissed."

Everyone gathered their books and personal belongings and shuffled out of the classroom—everyone except Shelley. She stayed in her seat with her eyes downcast.

I walked over to her desk and sat down in the one next to her. "It's your true story, isn't it?"

She looked up and met my gaze. "Yes, but no one has ever believed me before. Do you really believe me?"

"Yes, I do. No one could write a story that vivid unless they had experienced it."

She continued pouring out her story to me. "My dad's a pastor. He's charming and charismatic, and no one has any idea what goes on behind closed doors at home. No matter what I do, I can't please him. And when he's angry at me, he takes off his belt and beats me over and over again."

"Have you told anyone?" I asked.

She laughed a knowing laugh. "Oh yes. My mother didn't believe me. She lives totally in denial and doesn't want anything disturbing her make-believe world. I tried telling my teachers, but I'm something of a rebel, and who's going to believe a rebellious teenager over a pillar of the community?"

Bitterness and disdain filled her voice, and I prayed silently, *Lord, what do I say to this hurting young woman?*

"Would you rather read another story at the end of the semester? I don't want you to be uncomfortable reading your essay aloud."

"No, I want to read this story—my story. Everyone will think it is fiction anyway. After all, isn't this a fiction writing class?"

"Yes, and I think we can bend the rules a little and let you read a true-life story instead of a made-up one. Your story has tremendous depth to it, and it's very well written."

Shelley was silent for a moment as she stared again at the desk. Then she said, "I'm graduating in May. This is my last semester."

"Congratulations," I replied with a smile. Then I became serious. "I can't begin to understand how difficult your childhood and teenage years were, but you will soon be on your own. You can move to a community where no one knows your father and no one knows your history. This college has prepared you to find a job of your choice—and you can start a new life."

Shelley met my gaze once again, and for the first time, I saw a glimmer of hope in her eyes.

"What has happened to you is in no way your fault, Shelley. What your father did to you was wrong and until he's willing to get some help, nothing will change. As long as everyone covers everything up, nothing will change. So you need to leave your past behind and get on with the rest of your life. Only God knows the wonderful things He has in store for you."

We both stood up to leave, sensing that our conversation had ended. I reached out and hugged this special college girl. She lingered in my arms, making me wonder if her hugs had been few and far between.

She walked to the classroom door and then turned and looked at me one more time. "Thank you for believing me. It means a lot."

Momentarily I stood there staring into the empty hallway, blinking back tears. Then I prayed, *Lord, please take Shelley under Your wings and provide her with the special life You have for her.*

⟶ WORDS FROM JEENIE ⟵

"Behind closed doors." The shame, abuse, and trauma that exhibited itself in an essay is one the world did not see. Rarely does an abuser do it in public. Presenting a good image is foremost—being delightful, fun, and trustworthy. The truth is, they often get by with it. Who would believe such a charming, charismatic person, especially a godly pastor, would do such a dastardly deed? As Shelley rightly stated, "No one."

Psalm 27:10 states: *Though my father and mother forsake me, the Lord will receive me,* and He did just that through Susan's encouragement and kind words. She let Shelley know she believed her story and that she could have a better life in the future. Susan became a Barnabas "Son of Encouragement" (Acts 4:36) to a needy and desperate student.

REFLECTION: Are your seeing signs that indicate your children/ teens are being affected by the violence they witness or have experienced?

PRAYER: *Lord, protect my children emotionally, physically, and spiritually. Help me to make wise choices. In Jesus' name we pray, amen.*

Nowhere to Go

The righteous cry out, and the LORD hears them;
he delivers them from all their troubles.
The LORD is close to the brokenhearted
and saves those who are crushed in spirit.

—PSALM 34:17–18

HOPELESSNESS HAS MOVED in. It greets you in the morning, says good night to you at bedtime, and has the audacity to invade your dreams. To avoid conflict, you're constantly walking on *eggshells*—your health is in jeopardy.

Domestic abuse becomes an emotional merry-go-round. You want out, but life at home improves. Days turn into weeks, and weeks turn into months without any altercations. Hope returns. Then without warning violence erupts once more. And hopelessness again clutches your heart.

When life hurts and dreams fade, the choices we make truly matter and can make a difference—whether we decide to return to school, find a job, or reach out for advice and help. The following stories shed insights on the choices some women made.

When Liddy asked, "Why does Abigail and Marie's mommy wear sunglasses all the time?" Liddy's mom knew something was wrong. Because of her work with Lutheran Social Services, she suspected physical abuse.

THE SUNGLASSES

M. E. HENRY

The apartment complex seemed like a great place to begin again, to create a sense of home for Liddy, age nine, and Oriole, age six, after my divorce. My girls were excited to move next door to friends their age. Often the four could be seen after school, playing on the swings or taking turns pushing and riding on the merry-go-round.

Yet Abigail and Marie seemed shy and reluctant to come over to play. They told Liddy and Oriole that their dad forbade any strangers in their apartment. I encouraged my two to be friendly, but not ask too many questions about the "no visit" mandate from next door.

One day Liddy said, "Abigail and Maria's mommy doesn't come out on the playground to watch us. It's so sad, and when she does come outside, she always wears sunglasses. Why does their mommy wear sunglasses all the time?"

I replied, "Some people have eye problems and can't be in bright light. Probably, Mrs. Bingham had some condition like that."

As October faded from red and orange to brown, the crisp air made neighbor conversations fewer and fewer. Yet, something about Sandy Bingham seemed to change like the weather. When she took her girls to school, she appeared hunched over, clutching her side, barely able to get in and out of the car.

I did not think much about all of this until late November. I was busy with my girls, my work at Lutheran Social Services, and the plans for Thanksgiving.

Then a week before Thanksgiving, I was in the basement doing laundry, and I heard raised voices and groans coming through the crawlspace to the Bingham's apartment. It was late and my children were in bed. As I continued to fold laundry, the low moans came again, then silence . . .

Two days later as I was taking my girls to school, Sandy stood on her back porch telling Abigail and Marie they had to walk to school since their dad had taken the car.

I offered to take the girls that morning, even though these kiddos attended a different school than mine. Sandy shook her head no and kept talking to her kids. Standing on their back porch, she trembled in the cold, fingering her dark sunglasses despite the gray, overcast sky.

As I pulled into the parking area of the apartment complex after work, Sandy sat on her back porch. Her girls were not around, and their car was still gone. She gestured to me as I parked my car and climbed out.

"Mrs. Henry, can I talk to you?"

I walked over and stood close to her. She was shaking. "Of course," I replied. "Come into my place and I'll make you a cup of coffee."

"No, no! I don't have time. Randy will be back soon, and I don't dare face him again until he calms down." She stood dressed in a thin cotton windbreaker with her sunglasses still resting on the bridge of her nose.

I noticed a bruise under one eye and a cut over the other. "Are you OK?" I asked.

"Well, yes and no. Randy got real mad last night—more mad than normal, and he started pounding on me with his fists. I'm worried that he is still mad and that he might take it out on the kids. I sent them over to my friend Eileen's house for tonight. I am on my way over there with clothes and stuff.

But I needed to ask you to tell your girls not to say nothing to Randy. You haven't seen us, and you don't know where we are. Nothing! 'Cause if Randy is still mad, he will come a-knocking and ask you. He's like that when he's been drinking."

"OK, but I can help you! I know about Rachel's House—a safe house for women and children who are victims of abuse. Do you want to know about it?"

"No, I don't know about it, but I gotta go. Promise me, you won't say nothing." With that, she bolted off my porch and ran out of the apartment parking lot.

I watched her run, like she was running for her life. . . . Maybe she was.

I walked to the sitter's house and got my kids. When we turned the corner, Randy Bingham stood in our front yard. He turned and glared at me. For one minute I froze, and then I leaned over to Liddy and whispered: "Take Oriole, and go in the backdoor. Don't ask me any questions. Here are the keys— go now!"

Liddy took the keys, headed around to the backdoor, and promised Oriole a snack.

Randy Bingham scowled at me. "Do you know where my kids are?" He yelled despite being less than three feet from me.

"No, I don't know where your kids are. I haven't seen them," I replied.

"I don't believe you! You know where they are. Your kids know!"

"No, we just got home ourselves. I have not seen your children," I responded calmly.

"I wanna talk to your kids. I wanna ask 'em myself!"

"No, I don't think that is a good idea. They have to do chores."

He took three steps toward me and raised a clenched fist. "I wanna talk to yer kids now!" he yelled.

I walked two steps backward away from Bingham and proceeded to move quickly around the side and up on the back porch.

Bingham ran into my backyard yelling.

I came into the kitchen and closed and locked the door. Liddy was pale. She had been watching all of this through the window. Oriole sat at the table, consuming cookies.

"I am going to call the police. I want you and Oriole to go upstairs. Don't come down until I call for you." I whispered to Liddy.

"C'mon, Oriole, let's go play upstairs. Bring your cookie."

Randy Bingham was arrested on disorderly conduct. He yelled, "I'm gonna get you and my no-good wife."

Bingham stayed in jail and didn't make bail. Two days later, Sandy returned to her apartment with her girls. I arranged with Lutheran Social Services to get a referral to Rachel's House for Sandy and her girls.

By the end of the week, Sandy and her girls were gone. Sandy's friend Eileen came by to say she was grateful for my kindness, but she was taking her family to Kentucky to her mom's home. I never saw Sandy again.

Sometime later I saw Eileen at the grocery store. The best news was that Sandy had learned to stand on her own. She divorced Randy. They were doing well, and Sandy was working. She had decided that being Randy's punching bag was the wrong message to send to her girls. It was a life lesson for my girls too.

☙ WORDS FROM JEENIE ❧

An abuser—abuses. Sandy's husband was not untypical, especially when he had a belly full of alcohol. He was ready to take his neighbor on, and undoubtedly would have if he was convinced she knew where his wife and children were. Even while being arrested, he threatened not only his wife, but his neighbor—vowing to "get them." Unfortunately, those were plausible threats.

Thank God for a neighbor who watched Sandy and was available when Sandy was distraught. For Sandy, her chosen solution was to move to a distant state and begin life anew, as she eventually did.

When Sandy's neighbor offered assistance (rides for the children and a woman's shelter), she was unable to accept, for fear of her life. Yet perhaps it gave her the courage to finally get help for herself and her daughters.

DETECTIVE TOM'S TIP:
CALLING THE POLICE

To make that phone call, the victim needs to be safely away from the person who is abusing her or them. It's extremely dangerous for the woman to make the call near the abuser where he can hear her. She needs to go to a neighbor or to another location of safety or use a cell phone out of his earshot.

She needs to feel empowered to tell what is going on with some level of confidence in the appropriate response from law enforcement. Out of fear and shame, victims of abuse may minimize what is happening. They don't want to admit a problem. They simply want the abuse to end.

The husband or boyfriend will try to turn the tables on her, accusing her of being abusive. What if there is physical violence: Was she slapped, punched, or kicked? Did he use a weapon? If she had to defend herself, what did she do? Did she take affirmative action? The job of law enforcement is to determine the primary aggressor.

In order to make the assessment, law enforcement should make efforts to develop a thorough and complete picture of what is going on. This includes talking separately with the victim and alleged perpetrator, questioning witnesses, and also speaking with children who may have been present. Text messages, voice mails, threatening letters, photographs, and journal entries kept by the victim may also be helpful in an investigation.

LISTEN—DO YOU HEAR HIS VOICE?
CHARLES R. BROWN

In the midst of the
insensitive, abrasive, disrupting
clatter of the day,
do you hear His voice?
When you run to the edge
of a cliff and cannot navigate
toward safety,
do you hear His voice?
As verbal abuse, insult, and injury
pound on your heart's door,
do you hear His voice?

He calls His sheep by name.
He calls you by name.
Yes. He knows your name.
He knows where you live,
how you live,
what makes you tick
and what ticks you off.
Listen.

Do you hear His voice?
Shhhh.
Cover your mouth.
Quiet your heart.
Bend your soul in awe
of the Gentle Shepherd.
He speaks to you.

Wanda's mother was not afraid to get involved when she saw an injured woman leaning against a building. She thought it was her Christian duty to help.

A BLOODY STREET FIGHT
WANDA J. BURNSIDE

One hot summer day when I was about ten years old, my dad was driving through town in Detroit, Michigan. Mama, my brother Rodger who was eight, and Regina who was six, were also in the car. We had just come from visiting friends, and we laughed and joked.

Suddenly Mama frowned and pointed at a woman leaning against a red-brick movie theater on Joy Road. "Look, she's bleeding! Stop the car! I'm getting out to help her."

Dad shouted, "Willie, what are you talking about? You don't even know what is going on! I'm not going to let you out of this car to get killed!" Mama gave him that look. He sighed and pulled into a parking place. We could see that the woman was really bleeding. She looked like she'd been cut or stabbed. She was crying and screaming about some man and how she wanted him to leave her alone. We children were scared, and we lay down on the backseat and cried.

When our car came to a stop, Mama opened the door, got out, and ran across the street. She jumped up on the sidewalk and approached the bleeding woman. "Honey, what happened to you?" Mama asked. "Let me help you . . ."

"No! Stay away! Please go awa-a-ayy," cried the woman, as she waved her hands at Mama, hoping to stop her. "Pll-eeaa-se!"

Mama reached her hands out to touch the woman. "You're bleeding! God, help this woman! Help us, Lord! Come on. . . . Let me help you. Let us take you to the hospital."

"No! No! No!" screamed the woman, shaking her head as she moved away from Mama. Mama kept holding out her hands to the woman, but the woman kept backing up.

Dad looked worried as he got out of the car. He shouted at Mama, "Willie, come back here!" But Mama did not come. "Honey, you don't know what you are doing!" He turned to us and said, "You children, stay right here." Then he crossed the street.

By then, other cars had stopped. People started gathering around the scene. In those days, in 1960, there weren't cell phones. However, someone must have run over to a payphone on the street and called the police.

Thank God they did because a big man in a white T-shirt and black pants suddenly came around the corner. He waved a beer bottle in one hand and a butcher knife in the other. "Hey! Stay away from my wife!" he bellowed. He slowly weaved his way back and forth on the sidewalk as he staggered over to our parents.

When Dad saw him coming, he shouted, "You're not supposed to beat your wife or any woman. Man, what is wrong with you?"

"S—! Who in h— do you think you are?" the man shouted. He slammed that empty beer bottle on the brick building and it shattered. He came after Dad and Mama with the broken bottle and knife!

My brother, sister, and I watched the whole thing from the backseat of our car. We were praying out loud and screaming.

Dad shouted, "Satan, leave us now!"

The man took another step and then fell backward to the ground.

We heard sirens, and two police cars swarmed around the man. Two officers jumped out, cuffed the man, and put him in their police car. An ambulance arrived and placed the woman in it. The other policemen talked to my parents. Then they walked over to our car and talked to us.

Dad and Mama got back into our car and pulled us all onto the front seat. They kissed, hugged, and held us. "Everything is OK. . . . Everything is OK," they said.

What a frightening experience!

✦ WORDS FROM JEENIE ✦

Times have changed! Fifty years ago, people felt it was their obligation to get involved. Take action. Some even said, "It's my Christian duty." Hmmm, sounds like Jesus.

It appears most often today people refuse to interfere. "It's none of my business," they say. So, they allow other people to be throttled, injured, or even killed. They pass on by, or worse yet, stand and watch—cell phone in hand.

It reminds me of the good Samaritan story in Luke 10:29–37. A battered and bloody man was robbed and left to die by the side of the road. A priest and Levite both passed, both men of God, who were too busy to help. But a despised and hated Samaritan stopped, bound the man's wounds, took him to an inn, paid for his care, and promised to return. Two thousand years later, we have good Samaritan laws in place in our society.

There is a current television show about whether or not people will show concern and get involved in certain situations.

It surprises me how many continue on their way just as did the Levite and priest.

I certainly do advocate being cautious if it is a dangerous situation. However, most things are not, and I applaud this family for jumping in to rescue.

The woman in the story was undoubtedly a battered wife and terrified for her life. Likely she had been threatened a number of times, suggesting that any call for help on her part would result in certain death. Thousands of women are held captive in their fears of termination and do not seek outside assistance.

Since Jesus recommended our getting involved, it should be taken seriously. See his command to us in Luke 10.

> But a Samaritan, as he traveled, came where the man was; and when he saw him, he took pity on him. He went to him and bandaged his wounds, pouring on oil and wine. Then he put the man on his own donkey, brought him to an inn and took care of him. The next day he took out two denarii and gave them to the innkeeper. "Look after him," he said, "and when I return, I will reimburse you for any extra expense you may have."
>
> "Which of these three do you think was a neighbor to the man who fell into the hands of robbers?"
>
> The expert in the law replied, "The one who had mercy on him."
>
> Jesus told him, "Go and do likewise"
> (Luke 10:33–37).

How do you handle the situation when your husband orders you and your daughter to get out of his house? Where do you go? Who do you turn to? This was the dilemma Danielle faced.

ANXIOUS FOR FREEDOM
DANIELLE CLARK

"Get out of my house!" Alan yelled as he stomped down the basement stairs to confront my daughter, Katy, and me. His anger had exploded at Katy earlier, so we felt the basement was the safest place to be until he calmed down. Unfortunately, we were wrong.

Alan and I had been married eight years by then, each one of them marked with extreme control and intimidation. If Katy and I did what he expected us to do and looked the way he wanted us to look to fit his country club lifestyle, Alan was happy. If not, he would reject and ignore us, or punish us in subtle ways.

That particular night he was mad at Katy because her bedroom was a mess. She was creative and unorganized, but I read that it was OK for a teen's room to be messy as long as they did their part to keep the rest of the house in order. It seemed like a battle that wasn't worth fighting, particularly given the constant criticism that flew in Katy's general direction on a daily basis.

I had never seen Alan so mad. When he yelled at us to get out of *his* house, I was genuinely terrified of what he might do if we didn't.

Trying to remain calm, I walked Katy past Alan, upstairs to her bedroom to pack an overnight bag. Then I grabbed some pajamas, toothbrush, and makeup and quickly escorted her to the car.

Driving down the tree-lined lane, I felt like I was on autopilot, surviving the moment, protecting my daughter, without my mind present. I didn't know where to go, who to call. How do you tell someone your husband kicked you out? Do we let him sleep it off and return home tomorrow? What might we face then?

It was the middle of December, snowy and cold. We didn't want to drive around all night, nor did I want to check into a hotel. I hated to bother any of my friends, few though they were. Living in an emotionally explosive environment, I learned to isolate from people who I felt didn't understand. All they saw was the charming *public* Alan. They found it impossible to believe he could be cruel.

In a panic, I called my best friend, Anna. They were decorating their Christmas tree, but she insisted we come anyway. When we arrived, Katy and I were emotionally exhausted. We sat at the kitchen table and talked a short time, then fell onto the guest bed for a fitful night of sleep.

The next morning Katy woke up and dressed for school like any normal day. We didn't talk much on the drive until she said, "Mom, did you see Alan's eyes last night? They were red . . . like the devil."

I was stunned silent. What could I say in response to *that*? The 30-minute drive felt like an entire day. I turned on the radio to fill the empty space with something other than fear and dread.

When we pulled up in front of the middle school, Katy hesitated before opening the car door. "Are we going home tonight?" she asked.

I could see the terror in her eyes—hear it in her voice. My mind was racing. What should I do?

I shrugged and said, "I'm not sure yet. I'll check things out and let you know when I pick you up, OK?"

She frowned and hopped out. I drove off, physically, emotionally, and mentally exhausted—and deathly afraid of seeing Alan. As a self-employed businessman, he often worked from home. What would I say if he was there? Would he yell at me, or try to hurt me?

Fortunately, the house was empty when I arrived. I spent the day in front of the television, watching movies and eating junk food. And I prayed, hoping with all my heart that we would work things out. If we didn't, where would Katy and I go?

When I picked Katy up from school, I said, "I didn't hear from Alan all day. I have to run a few errands, and then we will go out for dinner. Sound good?" She nodded, looking relieved.

Because Katy's door upstairs had an Amish wood lock that wasn't all that reliable, I had her sleep on the pullout sofa in the basement so she could lock the door and feel as safe as possible.

Alan didn't come home until late. I prayed he would leave us alone, and he did. The next morning he showered, dressed, and left the house without speaking to me, and I was relieved.

Katy and I spent several weeks walking on eggshells, anxious about upsetting Alan and potentially pushing him over the edge. We never talked about the night he threw us out again. We just stuffed the fear and pain deep inside with the numerous wounds we buried for years.

Some days it felt like everything was OK, but underneath bubbled an unspoken terror. What was Alan capable of doing if he got that angry again? Or angrier?

I hadn't worked outside the home for five years, and I had no real desire to do so, but I began to wonder if I should get a full-time job. Early in our marriage when I went back to work temporarily, Alan cut my household allowance by the amount I earned, so it didn't seem worthwhile for me to go back to work.

For the time being, Katy and I felt stuck, but I never stopped praying that God would release us from the emotional and psychological abuse. I began to count the days until Katy would leave for college. Maybe then we'd both be free.

⚜ WORDS FROM JEENIE ⚜

Victims of abuse often live in fear. Fear keeps people stagnated and in a frozen state. Instilling fear in the victim is a tool the abuser uses to maintain control.

It takes courage and a great deal of planning for a victim and her family to launch onto a new and difficult path. If a person chooses to move ahead, hopefully she will eventually be rewarded for the hard work.

I've asked many fearful clients in therapy, "With hard work, are you able to rebuild your life at your present age? Or if you wait, will you be able to do it in five years? How about ten years?" Most understand that prolonging the process will be destructive.

Many years ago Suzanne came to me in therapy after recently leaving her husband and filing for divorce because of his abuse. She had five children. Her husband agreed for them to remain in the home until the last child graduated from high school. He paid the mortgage, the gardener, and the housekeeper as well as a hefty amount of child support. Per the divorce agreement, there was no spousal support.

Suzanne was a brilliant woman, and I urged her to think about going to college and preparing for a career. The money would run out in about five years, and she would no longer have lodging. "Suzanne," I urged, "you could attend college full-time, earn a degree, and be in a professional job before your children graduate from high school." My advice, however, fell on deaf ears.

Fear keeps people stagnated and in a frozen state. What many do not realize is that everyone has experienced fear and trepidation when launching onto a new and difficult path. If a person chooses to move ahead, they will eventually be rewarded for the hard work.

Psalm 37:23 says: *The LORD makes firm the steps of the one who delights in him.* He opens doors.

REFLECTION: Do you feel like you are wandering in a cycle of abuse? Are you confused about where to go to find help?

PRAYER: *Lord, deliver me from the pit of hopelessness. Give me courage and a new determination to change my circumstances. In Jesus' name we pray, amen.*

CHAPTER 7

Reality Check

Have no fear of sudden disaster or of the ruin that overtakes the wicked, for the Lord will be at your side and will keep your foot from being snared.
—PROVERBS 3:25–26

MAYBE YOU HAVE thought, *I wish my husband's verbal and physical abuse didn't control my life.* You know that friends and family are concerned. But wishing is not going to change your circumstances. Reality whispers, *Your life and health are being threatened. Courage shouts, It's time to take action!* Reality has a partner called truth. While reality reveals facts, truth confirms them. No one is going to tell you and your children to stay in an unsafe situation, but making a safe escape requires planning. It's time to take hold of wisdom's hand and believe that God has created you for a special purpose, and He will help you fulfill that purpose if you will only ask and depend on Him through the support of those who offer professional resources and safety planning.

The following stories demonstrate how reality, wisdom, and courage changed lives.

God uses brokenness and suffering to achieve His greater purpose in Mary's story.

MY STORY
DR. MARY M. SIMMS

Growing up in one of the roughest areas of New York, Bedford-Stuyvesant in Brooklyn, I experienced firsthand the sounds of violence, hopelessness, and despair at an early age. My family lived in fear of the daily crime and poverty that filled our lives. Drug dealing and using, gang violence, drive-by shootings, domestic violence, burglaries, rapes, and all sorts of violent and petty crimes were a daily occurrence in our neighborhood. Our lives were filled with the kind of ills that keep people chained to a life of poverty, violence, and abuse.

One night when I was five, gunshots thundered through our living room. "What is that noise that sounded like a big bang?" I asked my seven-year-old sister as I was awakened from a sound sleep.

"Don't go out there. Stay in our bedroom!" Jacquie screamed as she shoved me under the bed. I shivered in terror. When we left for school the next morning, we could see the telltale signs of violence left by the blood that had been spilled on the sidewalk the night before. Unfortunately, this became an all too familiar scene.

Another time, I remember walking home from school with Jacquie and Mom. As I started to open our apartment door, we heard our police dog barking loudly. My sister screamed, "Don't go in there! The door has been forced open!"

Terrified, I ran upstairs to the second-floor apartment where my aunt and uncle lived. Mom and Jacquie stayed downstairs to talk to the police. When my sister called up to me, "You can come home now, Mary," I pretended I did not hear her because I did not want to go home. I did not feel safe. I found out later blood was splattered throughout the house because our large dog bit the burglar several times as he ran, trying to find a way out of our home. That was just one of many times our house was robbed in the middle of the day.

Fear and terror gripped me almost daily. Dad was stabbed on two occasions, and fighting often broke out in the neighborhood. Living with fear and anxiety was what I knew as a child. I was always afraid that Dad would not come home because he might be hurt or killed.

Back then, our neighborhood was one of the hardest, roughest, and most unforgiving areas of New York City. Most people who left did so by way of death, drugs, or detention. Although Mom was married to Dad, more often than not, she was a single parent who carried the family both emotionally and financially. Dad was an alcoholic, and when he drank he always projected blame and anger on Mom.

I remember one incident when Dad had Mom pinned in a corner. "Daddy, Daddy," I screamed, "please don't hurt Mommy! Being older, my sister yelled, "Stop!" as I jumped in between them, trying to protect Mom. Jacquie didn't want me hurt.

Dad was not a bad man. He had a proud heritage as an African American military man. He was part of the 761st Tank Battalion, the legendary all-black tank unit known as the Black Panthers, who became famous for their heroic efforts during World War II. But Mom said after he came home from the war, he was never the same.

As staff sergeant he had experienced all kinds of atrocities in combat. One of the most traumatic was when he saw the decapitation of a good friend while engaged in battle. His friend was only 19 years old at the time. It wasn't until many years later, when I became a clinician, that I realized my father had suffered from post-traumatic stress disorder (PTSD) and turned to alcohol as a way of coping. And like many who use alcohol or other substances to ease their pain, he became physically abusive to Mom when he drank. Yet, he would not acknowledge or admit he needed help.

Like many families who live with abuse, we were tired of living that way. Mom did not know what to do, but God always has a way of working things out. In this case, it came by way of a letter from Louisiana.

Mom told Dad, "My sister's ill and asked me to come help take care of her."

"You're not going anywhere. I want you to stay right here. Don't you dare leave!" Dad threatened.

"Girls, we're leaving, and we are going to visit my sister who is very ill," she quietly told us one day. Both Jacquie and I did not have to be convinced—we were past ready and willing! So we decided to leave our painful life behind and move to a safer, more peaceful place. I was 12 years old at the time and my sister was 13 when we made our escape plan.

We left New York with few resources. All Mom had was an active prayer life and a determination to seek a better life. She cashed in her life insurance policies and hid our meager belongings in a locker at Penn Station until the day we took the train to Louisiana.

Although Mom was contemplating returning to Brooklyn after helping her sister, another sister, who lived in Arizona, called. "I think going back to Brooklyn would be a bad decision for you and the girls. What kind of a life did you have there? Why don't you come to Tucson and live with me?"

So, with the support of my aunt and her family, we made the move to Tucson. Shortly after that and only in his 40s, Dad had a stroke as a result of the alcoholism and stayed in a rehabilitation institution for seven years. He stayed sober for a long time, and we started communicating. Unfortunately, he went back to the same environment and set of friends who he used to drink with, and the drinking started again. He died shortly before his 54th birthday.

When we settled in Tucson, Mom went back to school and obtained her nursing credentials, so that she could support us as a single parent. Our lives changed drastically after that. Mom got a good job, and my sister and I attended college. After getting married and starting my family, I went on to obtain two master's degrees and a PhD. I often think about my difficult beginnings and marvel at how a poor little girl from Bedford-Stuyvesant became an empowered, educated woman of God who is no longer a victim, but now works with victims and broken people to help them find their purpose and destiny. It happened by the grace of God and with the support of a strong mother who had the courage and faith to get us out of a difficult environment.

⚘ WORDS FROM JEENIE ⚘

Mary's need to protect Mom, even though she was a small child, is one that is often demonstrated in an abusive home. It appears that the intervention lends itself more to the personality of the child. Mary dove in, yet her older sister was fearful. The fact remains, however, no youngster is capable of standing up to an adult—physically or emotionally. This is also often true for teenage boys who may intervene in an abusive relationship to protect the mother.

A number of years ago I counseled male youths who were incarcerated. Because they were not of legal age, they were kept in a juvenile facility. Working as an individual therapist, I learned a great deal about the streets, their criminal lifestyles, drugs, alcohol, and abuse. I also learned about the lives of their parents—many of whom were also incarcerated. Sadly, many of the youth robbed, sold drugs, raped, murdered, and copied the ways of many of their fathers, mothers, and ancestors. Through the years I have continued to pray for them.

In Mary's story, the courage of her mother paved the way for Mary's future. Because her mother decided to move out of state, earn her nursing degree, and raise her girls, her daughters followed in her footsteps Her choices helped her daughters choose a fulfilled, emotionally stable, and spiritually healthy lifestyle.

We are often given chances to plant seeds in the lives of those we are teaching, counseling, sharing, and praying with. And occasionally God gives us a glimpse of how He has watered those seeds and how they have grown.

PLANTING SEEDS
DR. MARY M. SIMMS

Watching Mom's level of integrity and tenacity sparked a burning desire and passion inside of me. That passion was the thing that drove me to prepare myself for the work that I was called to do—that of inspiring purpose and destiny into the lives of others. My first professional job out of college was working as a career counselor at a local university. It was my job to help people match their gifting and talents with the right major, which would eventually lead them to the career of their choice. One of the common themes that I saw was that many people had no idea what they wanted to do in terms of a career choice. Many were going to school just because their parents told them they needed to get a higher education. Some had so much emotional baggage that they could not even focus on a career choice. I learned early on that if I helped them with their emotional issues, they could focus better and felt more freedom to see clearer and make better choices.

Feeling a call on my life to go deeper in helping people by integrating biblical principles with psychological truth, I went back to school and got two master's degrees, one in pastoral counseling and the other in marriage and family therapy. Years later I went back and also received my PhD in counseling as well. Opening a private practice with a Christ-centered emphasis that combined biblical principles with psychological truth would enable me to pour my life into others and help people live the life God intended for them to live.

A number of years ago I counseled a young man I'll call Jim. He was 16 years old and involved in gang-related activities. His parents were loving parents, but they lived in a troubled area in Southern California. Dad and Mom were always working, so they were not always available to monitor Jim's behavior. This young man was easily influenced, got in with the wrong crowd, and started living his life by identifying with young men his age who often expressed themselves with a tremendous amount of anger.

In one of our sessions Jim said, "You're wasting your time. My parents want you to fix me, but I'm going to do whatever I want to do."

"Do you feel good when you are hurting others?" I asked.

"Not really," he reluctantly answered.

"How about when you hurt yourself?" I asked.

"I'm still young," he said, "I have plenty of time to turn my life around."

I don't think he realized the path he was on was leading to destruction for both himself and others around him.

He was confrontational, abusive, and defiantly violated the rights of others. He was also failing in school. I finally became so frustrated that I drew a picture of a jail cell and a cemetery and tried some reality therapy on him.

I pointed to that picture and said, "That is where you are headed, young man, if you don't make a decision to change your life!"

He did not respond to me, nor did he seem shocked, so I certainly did not believe that he took in anything I said. One day when he came in, he seemed locked up inside and appeared so angry and sullen that I did not think our sessions made any difference at all. He stopped coming to see me after that. Although I prayed for him, I did not think my work would bear any fruit.

Then, one day about five years later, I was having a particularly discouraging day when I saw a young man sitting in my waiting room. I looked inquisitively at him because he did not have an appointment.

"Do you remember me, Dr. Simms?" Since he was clean-shaven and well-groomed, I did not recognize him. "I used to come see you with my parents. They forced me to come, and I hated those visits. I know I gave you a really hard time."

I suddenly realized this was Jim. "Yes, I remember how difficult you were. I didn't think you heard a thing I said."

"Since that time I have turned my life around with God's help—and yours. I am now a youth pastor, and I came to thank you for the role you played in impacting my life."

What he didn't know was that I wanted to thank *him* for coming back to say thank you on that particularly difficult day!

I no longer wonder why God allowed me to grow up in such a hostile environment in one of the roughest areas of New York, Bedford-Stuyvesant. My background has given me insight, passion, and compassion. It is my prayer to help others experience the hope and life that anyone can have with a belief in themselves, a vision for where they are headed, and an uncompromising faith in a living and loving God.

⚜ WORDS FROM JEENIE ⚜

Mary touched this young boy's life, and five years later she saw the rewards of her work. Most of the time, I'm convinced we never have the privilege to know how our lives or words have an impact on others for the good. But occasionally, God gives us the joy of knowing. The same is true with friends and family who may be in abusive relationships. Simply saying, "I am concerned for your safety" and "You don't deserve to be treated this way" may open the door for future conversations when a victim of abuse is ready to disclose what she is going through.

When I was in high school, I vividly remember the day I spoke to a girl about the love of Christ. She laughed at me. As I left, I wondered whether I should have kept my mouth closed. Months later a different student approached me and asked if I remembered the day I witnessed to the unreceptive girl. Of course I did. It had been painful. "Well, I was listening," she said, "and I liked what you said. So I have invited Jesus into my life. Thank you for what you did."

In my counseling office the therapists often talk about the fact that with some clients it can be difficult, and sometimes we wonder if we are getting through. At times, it can be discouraging, and it's not unusual to think, *What's the use?* Even so, we remind each other that we are doing this as "unto the Lord" as Scripture states; and even if we do not see the results we would hope for, we trust God for the outcome. Often we are planting seeds that will take root and grow in time.

As believers, we have not only the privilege, but the responsibility, to speak to others about Christ. We do not, however, need to do the work of the Holy Spirit. Our job is to be a witness and remain faithful.

While writing this book, my new computer was giving me fits. I called for tech support and spoke to a young man in another country. He was kind and helpful, fixing my problem and also checking out the entire computer system for more than an hour.

During our conversation, he asked about my book and profession and seemed interested. I prayed, "Lord, I'd like to witness to this man, but I don't know what to say. So, if You want me to do it, then open the door."

Near the end of our time together, he complimented me about being patient, kind, and gracious. At that point, I called him by name (written on my screen) and said, "I am a Christian. I'm wondering if there is anything I can pray about for you?" After a pause, he responded. "Just asking me is enough." I then told him I would pray for him, and he thanked me profusely. I have no idea how God will choose to use this in his life, but I am confident God will.

There is a Christian song entitled, "Little Is Much When God Is in It." How true!

DETECTIVE TOM'S TIP:
LAW ENFORCEMENT CHECKLIST FOR PERPETRATOR:

This is a checklist to determine how dangerous the perpetrator is. We start with the childhood of the perpetrator and work forward.

1. Look at childhood offenses: cruelty to animals, siblings, or parents. More often this involves animals that are weaker than the child, more vulnerable. Arson: destructive behavior. Often start acting out during formative years, ages 10 or 11.

2. Previous relationships: Look for a history of abuse, restraining orders, police reports. These give, for the police,

a barometer of the current situation. The man is usually stronger in adulthood, and the tendency to dominate the less vulnerable is carried over from childhood where he dominated animals.

3. Stressors leading to violence are also on the checklist:
   A. Financial issues
   B. Problems with kids
   C. Relationship is moving toward disillusionment: "I'm going to live somewhere else" or "I can't take this anymore," verbalizes the female. The abuser realizes he is losing the woman. This is a big one.

Sometimes women think they deserve the mistreatment, but they never deserve the abuse. It is not their fault!

When Marigold was at the end of her rope, she sought guidance from a wise counselor who helped her see the reality of her circumstances.

THE DECISION
MARIGOLD

Seeking a solution to our marriage troubles, I enlisted our pastor's help in persuading Argyle to accompany me to our denomination's counseling center. During a private session, I told the counselor how Argyle tried to trap me with my own words and refused to help around the house or engage in meaningful conversation. Instead of lowering the newspaper when I tried to talk, Argyle would insist, "I can hear you."

Eventually my husband withheld even basic information about appointments, phone calls, messages to me from other people, and upcoming events to which I was expected to accompany him. I told the therapist that Argyle often seemed irritated or angry, even though I hadn't meant to upset him. No matter how many different ways I tried to convey my intentions, he would interpret them negatively and respond in anger.

"When I vowed 'Till death do us part,' I meant it," I said. "I know I'm not perfect, but no matter how hard I try, I can't seem to fix our marriage. I don't know what to do."

The counselor looked me in the eye. "You need to consider leaving."

I gulped. Our denomination didn't believe in divorce. "You know I can't do that. I'd lose my job at church as women's ministries director."

"I've noticed the involuntary twitch in your arm," he responded. "Your body and spirit are breaking down from the stress."

"But ever since Argyle was laid off two years ago, the home-based business he started hasn't done well," I explained. "I'm supporting us both now."

The counselor wasn't dissuaded. "Marigold, if your daughter was going through the same thing, what would you tell her?"

I smiled wryly. "You know how to hit below the belt. I'd tell her the same thing you're telling me. OK, I'll pray about it."

"While you're praying," he said, "you *must* give serious consideration to your own needs. Otherwise you won't make it. In fact, if your husband is unwilling to change and you don't leave, you'll wind up institutionalized or dead."

I already knew I was going to die. For several years I'd experienced increasing physical symptoms: the involuntary twitching, plus heart palpitations, candidiasis, pleurisy, unexplained skin rashes, digestive upsets, respiratory infections. . . . Now new symptoms had developed. I realized that since I viewed death as my only escape, my body was about to provide it. I even planned the funeral in my mind—the location, the songs, the sermon I'd preach via prerecorded videotape.

Then to my dismay, God told me I couldn't take that way out. I realized if nothing improved, my only alternative was to separate, but then I'd lose everything. So I became more assertive, and in the space of a year, Argyle and I went to seven counselors; but the abuse escalated. He would accidentally hit or bump me hard. He insisted it was unintentional, but I wasn't sure I believed him.

I had read that deliberate silent treatment constituted a kind of abuse called *crazy-making*. So, when out of deep concern for my safety one of the counselors warned me that Argyle had admitted he was trying to drive me crazy, I wasn't surprised. Around that time, a Christian psychiatrist diagnosed Argyle with a mental illness. That answered a lot of my questions.

But the senior pastor, who was also my boss and the head of the elder board Argyle served on, didn't believe the diagnosis. He told me to get my act together and work out my differences with Argyle because he couldn't have someone on staff whose marriage wasn't solid.

Soon after that, we received a cutoff notice from a utility company. I learned that Argyle, who had been in charge of our finances for decades, was failing to pay bills on time. With the pastor's assistance I took over bill-paying responsibilities and our joint checking account. But the action went against my lifelong training to obey my husband as head of the home. I struggled with guilt.

The day after Christmas, a house fire left us with $13,000 in damage. Three weeks later, I learned that Argyle had neglected to pay our homeowners insurance premium and hadn't informed me of the bill so I could pay it. The fire wasn't covered.

At tax time, Argyle was extremely belligerent and uncooperative. When he dumped a year's worth of papers on the dining table and took three days to come up with profit/ loss figures, I discovered he kept no books for his business

Late on April 15, Argyle had the tax form ready. Feeling pressured, I signed it. Then I worried. We lived in a community property state. If we were audited and discrepancies were found, I'd be held equally responsible.

Meanwhile, Argyle stopped opening his personal bills, and bill collectors were calling. He maxed out our joint credit card with business expenses. No repairs were being made to the fire damage.

I sought counsel from Christian financial experts and learned I had two options for financial protection: divorce or legal separation. Divorce was out of the question, so I filed for legal separation—which is like a divorce for people who object on religious grounds to a full dissolution. I wept as I signed the papers.

Counselors thought the action might motivate positive change in Argyle. Instead, his behavior worsened, and he spread untruths about me. Few people checked with me for clarification. Some would avert their eyes when passing me in the church hallway. I longed to set the record straight, but I knew I should trust God for my defense since speaking out would hurt too many people.

When Argyle moved out nine months later, I resigned my church staff position. Now alone, unemployed, and spurned by former friends, I wondered why God had not answered my desperate pleas for help.

WORDS FROM JEENIE

Often, because of what the abuser has put them through, women believe—as I did—that if we try harder, pray more, acquiesce, excuse, and put up with the abuse, somehow a horrible marriage will work out. As in Marigold's story, seldom does it survive.

Abuse comes in all forms, and too often verbal and emotional abuse are often discounted. Only when a person is sent to the hospital for stitches and broken bones is it looked upon as abuse. Almost daily in my private practice as a therapist I see abuse and the vast majority is not physical. Abuse in any form is unacceptable!

Argyle began in small, irritating ways—keeping secrets— not telling his wife when someone left her a message, or not mentioning appointments and upcoming events they should attend together. He began the isolation process to cut her off.

Because her husband had a failing home business, Marigold needed to work full-time and carry the financial load. My guess is that he contributed little to nothing. In fact, she later found out he was keeping no records and realized they could be in trouble with the IRS. Heartsick after a home fire, she realized Argyle had not paid the homeowners insurance premium. He defiantly dumped a year's worth of receipts on her desk and abdicated himself of the responsibility.

Even though Marigold worked diligently to get them on track economically, she felt guilty taking control of the finances, thinking she was taking away Argyle's headship of the home. Although the husband is scripturally head of the house, the Bible does not spell out the exactness of the role. I suggest to clients that whoever has the best business sense should be in charge of the household monies. Obviously Argyle was not the one, as he maxed out credit cards and neglected to pay bills.

When a counselor suggested that she separate or divorce, she knew she would no longer have a job at the church. Sadly, her pastor made it quite clear that would be the case. After signing the separation papers, Marigold had to resign from her church position. She stayed in the church and tried to hold her head up high in spite of the lies being spread by her husband and the pain of being ignored by many in the congregation.

Often we cannot control what happens to us; however, we can control our responses. My suggestion to Marigold would have been to change churches, friends, and even communities and create a new life elsewhere. She needed a new start and space to begin the healing process. We can see that later in this book as we will pick up her story.

REFLECTION: Do you understand that domestic abuse is not your fault? What steps can you take for a new start?

PRAYER: *Lord, I humbly bow before You and ask for wisdom. Help me not to deny the abuse I live with. Father, I look to You for my deliverance.*

CHAPTER 8

Taking Off the Mask

Do not lie to each other, since you have taken off your old self with its practices and have put on the new self, which is being renewed in knowledge in the image of its Creator.

— COLOSSIANS 3:9–10

THE MAN IN the Iron Mask is a name given to a prisoner, arrested as Eustache Dauger in 1669 and held for a period of 34 years in a number of jails, including the famous French Bastille. He died on November 19, 1703, during the reign of King Louis XIV of France. We don't know his true identity because whenever he was brought out of his cell, his face was hidden by a mask of black velvet cloth.

The philosopher Voltaire claimed the prisoner who wore an iron mask was the older, illegitimate brother of Louis XIV. In the late 1840s, the writer Alexandre Dumas elaborated on the theme in his book, *The Vicomte de Bragelonne*, but made the prisoner a twin brother of the cruel King Louis XIV. This book has served as the basis—often loosely adapted— for many film versions of the story.

Women and children who are suffering under the yoke of emotional and physical abuse often wear masks. Shame, and the sheer weight of the abuse they suffer, prevents them from wanting anyone to know what their life is like inside their own home. They cover bruises with makeup and long sleeves, and they smile as if everything in their life was going smoothly. If you are wearing a mask and need your situation to change, consider seeking help from a friend, doctor, pastor, or counselor.

After suffering in an abusive marriage for more than 12 years, Diane took off her mask at a conference and allowed Christian brothers and sisters to comfort her and pray for her.

THE COLOR OF LIFE
DIANE WILLIAMS

Dressed in black pants and a gray sweater, I stood weeping in a small room off the side of the large conference area. Four men and women surrounded me and prayed over my broken and bruised heart. One man said, "God sees you. He knows your pain. He has been with you all along, and He wants you to know that you don't have to be strong anymore. There are people who are safe to share your pain with. Open up. Ask for encouragement and support."

Surviving an abusive marriage for more than 12 years, I was worn out. It was difficult to sustain energy to fake a smile throughout the ten-hour writers conference days. Who was I to write a book when my personal life was a mess? *Why didn't the years of individual counseling change things? If my husband, Mike, loved me like he said he did, why did he treat me like my thoughts and feelings didn't matter? Like I didn't matter?*

Six years earlier I had experienced a deep depression where I isolated myself from everyone in my family. Mike was respected as a Christian businessman. I thought no one would believe what he was really like at home. If I told them, they might think I was lying. Everything looked so perfect on the outside. What could I do?

Mike's first wife left after 16 years of marriage, citing he was emotionally and psychologically abusive, but I didn't believe her. The man I dated treated me like a princess. Before we married, I could never have imagined my life, and my daughter's life, would end up in such a dysfunctional mess.

As the small group of men and women continued to pray over me, my body shook with grief as I sobbed so hard I didn't think I could ever stop. I was embarrassed, but it felt good to finally be heard, *believed*, and prayed for. I had approached two different pastors in prior years for help, but both insisted I submit to my husband, "cook a good dinner," and all would be well.

Nothing could have been further from the truth.

Little did I know how my life as an emotionally abused woman would change after that powerful time of prayer. Coming out of that sparsely decorated room, I felt physically lighter, like a weight had been lifted off my heavy heart. A few weeks later I went forward at church for prayer and fell into a ball on the floor, weeping for nearly 40 minutes after the service, grieving the criticism, control, and deceit I had lived with for so long.

One day at a time I prayed for courage and began to selectively open up to women who I sensed would hear me and support me in my pain. A couple of women I opened up to did not give me the encouragement I desperately needed. The pastor's wife even told me she felt it was my own unforgiving heart that was holding my marriage back from being blessed by God. She wounded me deeply, which caused additional pain, but I did *not* give up.

God eventually led me to a wonderful Holy Spirit-filled church with a dynamic support and recovery program where the counseling pastor listened and empowered me to speak

ke, both in and out of marital counseling. After one
int counseling, the pastor sensed what my heart knew
ig. Mike had no desire to work on our marriage. He was
unded, broken man who had no interest in changing or
coming a more loving human being.

Praise God for that counseling pastor and for the women
who have come into my life since then. It's taken three and a
half years of active counseling and selective sharing with other
women at church to fully grasp the truth of my marriage and
work through the rest of the grief and wounding that I held in
my heart for so long.

Mike and I are legally separated. I'm uncertain what God's
will is at this point. I only know that I have an increasing
number of supportive, loving, godly men and women who are
lifting me in prayer and in friendship. And I have never felt
more free—fearful at times—but free.

It all started with the powerful prayer of those faithful
people who reiterated God's promises to me, promises that are
true for every woman like me. God loves us. He sees us. He
knows everything that is happening in our lives. He has been
with us all along.

There *are* safe people to open up to who will believe us
and support us. It's OK to ask for help. And when we share the
truth with people who *don't* support us, we can give them to
God and move on.

I find as I read the Bible more, I feel closer to God, and He
seems to send more people to encourage and support me. And
the best part is, they want to know the *real* me. That's great
news for those of us who hid so long we forgot who we were.

Apart from my husband, I'm discovering hobbies and
interests that I forgot I even enjoyed. My heart is at peace, and
my life is moving slowly forward.

A gray veil no longer covers my mind. My heart feels so much more than black and blue. I finally get to use the whole box of crayons and color my life as God intended. I think I'll toss the dark colors in the trash. Authentic living leads to a colorful life, filled with boldness and beauty. That's the life I plan to live.

⁓ WORDS FROM JEENIE ⁓

I've had two precious experiences of people praying over me. Like Diane, I was going through an unwanted divorce. A group was in my home, and as I was preparing coffee in another room, I heard them, one-by-one, holding me up to the Lord in prayer. Another time at a women's retreat, I spoke briefly with the keynote speaker. She asked about my situation. I gave a thumbnail sketch, and she took me in her arms and prayed. Both these instances still bring tears because of the love and caring by the body of Christ that I experienced.

There is a lot of free and unwanted advice in the world. Sadly, Diane was on the receiving end. We must be extremely careful what we tell people because only they know the extent of their pain. Unsolicited advice is often destructive, dangerous, and heartbreaking.

Yet, it is imperative in my view that we listen to truth and warning in our lives—as long as it comes from a caring and factual source. Regrettably, the reports from Mike's former wife about the emotional and psychological abuse she suffered during their marriage may have been a red flag that Diane missed. Often, if a person has been abusive in one relationship, chances are very high that he will abuse again. If anyone hears those words, no matter how wonderful the husband-to-be appears, take them to heart. Seldom, if ever, do they change.

Grieving over a lost marriage is, per studies, more difficult than the death of a spouse. When there is a death, the grieving widow was loved to the end. People send sympathy cards, shed tears at the funeral, bring casseroles, and keep in touch for some time. Not so with divorce. Often the separated or divorced person is isolated, and sometimes condemned. Mourning the marriage, therefore, takes on a very different meaning.

Diane learned to stay away from people who were criticizing and judging, even if they were pastors, pastors' wives, or highly thought of members of the congregation.

She found a place of support and healing and has been able to establish a new lifestyle.

Joan was a successful business administrator, who loved her job. No one would suspect the horrific home life that took place behind her mask.

JOAN'S STORY
DR. MARY M. SIMMS

Joan entered my counseling office looking poised and professional in her business suit and heels. I learned she was a 55-year-old school administrator whose children were grown. She and her husband had been married 25 years and were now empty nesters.

She looked a little nervous as she began talking. "I came to you because my medical doctor told me that I need to talk to someone about how to deal with the stressors in my life. Like everyone else, I have the normal stresses such as balancing full-time work and family life."

As I talked with Joan, I found out that her medical condition was so severe that her stress was manifesting itself physically. She was breaking out with hives and welts all over her body. I wasn't fooled by her making light of the situation. I asked, "What is going on in your life that is causing you so much stress?"

Joan replied, "I guess it is just the stress of living in an urban community."

After that evasive answer, I had her talk about her responsibilities at work. I discovered she loved her job, and it seemed to fit her like a glove. I tried a different approach. "So, how is your home life going?"

"All right, I guess," she reluctantly reported.

"What does that mean?"

"Well, my husband says I'm controlling."

"Just how controlling are you?" I asked.

"Well, I really don't know, because I pay all the bills and then we fight about me keeping some money for myself to take care of my personal needs."

"So what is wrong with that?"

"He says I am being selfish. I want to be fair, because he keeps telling me that he is the head of the household."

"So is your husband a good provider?" I asked.

"Well, uh, he has not worked in a long time. He has problems getting work, and the economy is bad right now."

"How long is a long time?"

Joan hesitated for a moment and then replied, "More than five years. He is right, you know, in that God did make him to be head of his household."

"So what does *headship* mean to you?" I asked.

She seemed puzzled at first, but then responded, "Well, God wants me to respect and trust his decisions."

"That's true if he is committed to leading responsibly and loving you as he should."

She paused, "Well, that is the problem. I don't think he makes good choices; and when he gets angry, he starts getting loud, and it gets scary. "

"What does that mean?"

She sheepishly admitted, "He threatens to hit me if I don't agree with him and do what he says."

"Has he ever hit you?"

She reluctantly replied, "Well, yes, just a few times."

"You know, one time is too many times!" I answered passionately. She nodded, but seemed too powerless and trapped to know what to say or do to change the situation. I continued, "Give me an example of something that has happened."

"One day I stopped at the mall to buy some shoes, so I was 30 minutes late getting home. I was afraid to tell him where I'd been, so I decided to lie and tell him I was working late.

"When I got home, he was angry. He told me that I had 30 seconds to explain where I was. I felt as though I was a small child, and I had done something horribly wrong. I certainly did not feel like I could be honest about stopping at the mall because if I let him know that I bought myself some shoes, he would have become more enraged."

"So what did you tell him?"

Joan said, "I told him I was working on a project at work that was due tomorrow. The moment I said that, he lunged at me and said, 'You f— b—! I know you are lying. I called the school and was told you left an hour ago.' Then he slammed me onto the floor."

As she recalled her story, she began to experience the emotional pain and trauma of it all over again.

"Were you hurt?" I asked.

"No," she answered, as the tears started to surface, "but I felt trapped with no way out."

"Did you call the police?"

"No, this was not the first time this type of thing happened. Normally, he would just go away and then come back and apologize for it later. Things would go along fine for a while until something triggered him, and the same thing would happen again."

"You could have been hurt badly," I answered.

Because of her fear and the amount of trauma caused to Joan by living with an abuser, she minimized the abuse by pointing out that the abuse only happened several times a year, and that it was her fault because she made him angry. After doing some teaching with her that it was never acceptable to resolve conflict with physical abuse, she began to see how she was minimizing the abuse. She realized she needed help to value herself and not minimize or normalize a situation that should never be part of a relationship.

After several more sessions on developing self-esteem and empowerment issues, I recommended that she reach out and get some additional help. She started attending a women's group at a domestic violence shelter and became more aware and understanding of what she was dealing with. At that point I saw her less frequently.

As she developed more confidence in her own voice, she began to visualize a life without abuse and started moving toward a legal separation.

⚞ WORDS FROM JEENIE ⚟

No one wants to believe she is an abusive relationship. Joan had great difficulty admitting to herself that the man she married was a controller, as well as an abuser. However, with professional counseling and the encouragement she received by joining with other survivors in a domestic violence support group, Joan learned about the unhealthy dynamics in her relationship and her options for moving away from the relationship.

Abusers are manipulative, projecting onto others their own issues, as in Joan's husband calling his wife controlling. I've had numerous men in my therapy office who use God's Word out of context to support their own dysfunctional issues. It would not surprise me if this husband, as well, lorded it over his wife regarding the spiritual injunction to be head of the house. This is certainly not what we see modeled in Scripture. Ephesians 5:25 states: "Husbands, love your wives just as Christ loved the church and gave himself up for her."

Many women can be in high positions at work, well thought of and respected, but live in fear at home. With time and appropriate support from others, victims of violence can move away from fear to a place of wholeness and healing.

DETECTIVE TOM'S TIP:
HOW TO LEAVE AN ABUSER:

1. Women have a foreboding of danger and need to have a plan of escape. The biggest mistake women make is a spontaneous decision. Women need a safe place to go.

   Example: A woman who was in a dating relationship had never given any indication she was going to dissolve the relationship. Then one evening she hinted that she was going to break up with her abuser while he was over at her apartment. He started crying. He seems laudable and childlike, so she told him he could spend the night. In the middle of the night he armed himself with a kitchen knife and stabbed her in her bed, killing her. He fled to another state but was apprehended.

2. A woman needs to stash some money away so she is not financially beholding to her abuser. She needs to put herself and her children in the position to survive financially once they have left. There are cases of women who made a break, but were unable to make it on their own financially, so they went back. At first the abuser may say, "Remember the fun we had at _____ ?" or "I'm sorry. I'll never do it again." Yet in time the abuse escalates, and some women were even killed.

3. A woman needs to develop a support system. She needs an adviser, particularly when children are involved. It can be a member of the clergy, a trusted adviser, a friend, or counselor—someone who will provide sage advice regarding domestic violence.

   Detective Tom advises: Do not go back! Often the victim misses the abuser. If she goes back, that is when the violence escalates. He looks at the victim as being weak if she comes back, and he is angry at her for leaving. Abusers love to play mind games. The victim may think, *I sent him a message when I left*, but it's not true. Abusers becomes bolder when the victim returns. Plus, it's harder to make the break the second time.

Polly was able to take off her mask after suffering emotional and physical abuse for four years thanks to an understanding brother and his wife.

A BROTHER'S ADVICE
HAZEL MORGAN

The day my sister-in-law, Polly, and her daughter came to visit we were shocked at her appearance. She was skin and bones and only weighed 85 pounds. She poured out her story to us.

"Shortly after meeting Roy at college, he graduated and moved to another state. I continued with my education and obtained my nursing degree. During our entire dating relationship, I only saw Roy on weekends when he was on his best behavior."

"I remember coming to your wedding. It was large with a beautiful reception," I said.

"Roy insisted that I become a Catholic before we married, so before our wedding I attended classes and became Catholic. My dad threatened not to come to the ceremony, but my mom smoothed it over, and he showed up to walk me down the aisle. I see now that Roy was controlling from the beginning of our relationship. Hindsight is always 20/20.

"The night of our wedding, I found Roy standing on the balcony of our hotel room in his underwear. He seemed irritated. I realized something wasn't right, but I thought he was just nervous, being a newlywed and all. And, Hazel, how could I face all those people who came to our wedding and brought those beautiful gifts if I backed out on my marriage?"

Polly went on to tell us about another incident early in their marriage when Roy dumped out all the drawers in the kitchen and threw the food in the refrigerator on the floor. "I had done something to make him mad, so I thought this was just a one-time incident." However, over the next four years, the abuse escalated from verbal call downs to hitting and physical injury.

"I thought having a child would solve our problems, so I was thrilled when I became pregnant. Unfortunately, the abuse continued. He said, 'You are too ugly and stupid to give birth to a normal child.' I felt trapped. I didn't know what to do."

Roy worked as an editor at the local newspaper, which was across the street from their bank, so Polly always gave him her paycheck to deposit each week. She didn't realize there was a problem until after her little girl, Laurie, was born, and Polly began to pay the medical bills.

Roy said, "You can't pay the hospital bill. There's no money in the checking account."

"I was in shock," Polly said. "Both of us made good money. How could he have spent all our money? As time went by, he drank more and more and became meaner. One night I fixed a spaghetti dinner. Apparently he wasn't in the mood for spaghetti, so he threw the serving dish against the wall. My parents were coming by, so I just left it there, hoping I could get some wisdom from them. However, they just looked at the mess, visited briefly with their granddaughter, and left."

Polly could tell her parents weren't going to help, so she decided to go to their priest. The night before, Roy had twisted the chain on the cross around her neck until it dug into her skin. She poured out her story to her priest, and he replied, "This is the cross you will have to bear." The priest ignored the ugly marks on her neck.

The abuse escalated to a point where she was often knocked out when Roy hit her. Although Roy had never harmed Laurie, Polly feared for her daughter's safety also. One evening when Polly was knocked out during a fight, she awoke on the floor and saw Laurie, standing in her crib screaming. Polly didn't know how long she had been unconscious, and Roy was nowhere in sight.

Polly realized she had to do something before he harmed Laurie, so she and Laurie got on a plane and came to visit Hank and me.

Hank took his sister's hands and said, "I would never tell anyone to get a divorce, but you need to get out of that house for a while and get your thoughts together to decide what you want to do. Let's talk to our parents and see if when you go back, you can move in with them for a while."

Everyone agreed, and Polly and Laurie moved in with her parents temporarily. "Roy called and said it would never happen again. He made promise after promise, but once I had gotten some distance between us, I realized it was all talk. If I went back, he would revert to the same abuse again."

When she was feeling better, she moved to a new town, rented an apartment, and got a job at the local hospital. At first she had no car, so she rode a bus to take Laurie to day care and then another bus to the hospital. Roy had visiting rights with Laurie, but he made the mistake of taking her to a tavern when she was nine years old. Laurie felt uncomfortable and told her mom she never wanted to see him again. His visiting rights were revoked.

Although money was tight for a while, Polly felt free. She no longer feared going home at night, and she moved on with her life.

❧ WORDS FROM JEENIE ❧

Even one controlling action in courtship is often the precursor to lifelong abuse. It may be ignored, smoothed over, rationalized, and justified. Insisting that Polly convert to Catholicism was a huge red flag furiously waving in front of her.

In therapy, I've spoken with countless clients about the urgent need to look for red flags in relationships. One pops up, and the victim may tell herself, *Well, no one is perfect,* or *I need to give a little,* or *I'm too picky,* etc. etc. The excusing begins. The problem is that as red flag after red flag springs up, more justifying takes over. Eventually, there are no more red flags, Sigh!

Such was the case of a young couple I saw in therapy. They were to be married within the month and came in for premarital counseling. I sensed there was something decidedly wrong with the groom-to-be. Later in the session, I looked him straight in the eyes and asked, "Are you in love with her?" After much hesitation, he quietly stated, "Well, I care for her." I continued to probe, "But are you in love with her?" He finally said, "No."

I looked at his fiancée and asked, "Did you hear what he just said? "Well, yes," she replied, "but we've ordered the cake and my dress is ready as are all the bridesmaids." I closed the session by saying, "Here's my card. I suggest you keep it, as I suspect you are going to need it."

Polly's dad was evidently not in favor of the wedding, as he stated he would not attend, but changed his mind. I'm wondering why her parents did not express their concerns over the forthcoming nuptials. It needed to be said only once. They, however, remained silent, and years later when Polly desperately needed help, they were unavailable.

It's sad to know that a man of the cloth, Polly's priest, would encourage her to continue to live in abuse. Yet, I've heard such suggestions from a number of ministers.

In Polly's story, we see an honest depiction of the spectrum of abuse that included verbal put-downs, destruction of property, financial abuse, abuse that escalated during pregnancy, and physical injury. The priest missed an opportunity to offer faithful guidance and support to a young woman in danger. It took a great amount of courage for Polly to break free and find peace for herself and her daughter.

I cherish the verse in Joel 2:25: *I will repay you for the years the locusts have eaten.*

And, He does!

REFLECTION: Do you hide the truth about your abuse? How can you begin to take off your mask?

PRAYER: *Lord, I seek Your presence. Help me to be honest with my friends and family. Help me to reach out to others for comfort and answers. In Jesus' name I pray, amen.*

CHAPTER 9

The Fallout of Abuse

When you pass through the waters,
I will be with you;
and when you pass through the rivers,
they will not sweep over you.
When you walk through the fire,
you will not be burned;
the flames will not set you ablaze.

—Isaiah 43:2

"I'M GOING TO kill everyone who was mean to me," wrote Eric Harris in his personal journal. He went on to state that he, with the help of Dylan Klebold, hoped to kill hundreds.

On April 20, 1999, on the campus of Columbine High School in Littleton, Colorado, they attempted to carry out their plan. They wore trench coats to hide automatic guns and carried duffel bags full of homemade bombs. Students and teachers hid in classrooms as shots echoed throughout the hallways. Their fallout of rage resulted in the deaths of 12 students and one teacher as well as 21 injured. It ended with their suicides.

After this tragedy stricter guns laws were passed, and tighter security on high school campuses have been implemented.

Every day in the US at least three women are murdered by their husbands or boyfriends. For those living with domestic violence, there is no shame in seeking help. It may even save the lives of you and your children.

Tim was unable to control his abuse toward his son until he discovered the roots of his anger and rage.

ROOTS OF RAGE
TIM WILLIAMS

What am I doing here? I thought to myself. I couldn't believe I, a pastor, was sitting in a therapist's office, and we were filling out paperwork reporting me to Child Protective Services because of my own behavior.

My son, Evan, was referred to a therapist because he had hit other children at the Christian school where he was in third grade. After a few sessions with the therapist, it came out that I had beaten Evan. Yes, it's true, I'm ashamed to say, I have sometimes become out of control with my anger and have hit Evan beyond what would be a normal spanking.

I deplore my behavior, I felt myself screaming inside, *It goes against everything I believe and stand for.*

I couldn't understand how I could get so angry and lose complete control of myself. It was like I was driven by some force. I'd wondered about that for years. Every time I lost control and beat my son, I promised myself it would never happen again. And then it did. Each time I became mired in my own guilt and shame.

I heard the therapist assuring me, "Since you are already seeking help through therapy, probably there will be no further action following an investigation by Child Protective Services."

"Well, I want this behavior of mine to stop. So whatever it takes, even the embarrassment of being reported." I replied.

After filling out the paperwork, the therapist called Child Protective Services, Though it was embarrassing, the officials came to interview me, interviewed my son at school, and placed my case on hold while I continued therapy.

I remember one session clearly. We explored my uncontrolled rage reaction when my son began to step out of line. As the therapist had me sit with that feeling, I felt like I became a little guy myself . . . and remembered being beaten much more brutally by my own father. Then I realized that my rage toward my son was actually my fear that he would get hurt much more brutally if he didn't behave properly.

"Ah, now I get it," I told the therapist. "My unresolved fear from my own father beating me senseless is behind my inability to control my anger toward my son."

As I continued to explore all this with the therapist, I found myself being more and more in control of my angry reactions. I also had people pray over me for healing of my own woundedness. I sensed a great release after this. I now have found other ways to deal with my fear and anger when my son misbehaves besides abusing him.

This was a totally embarrassing part of my life, but I'm glad I have moved forward and explored it in therapy. I think in the end, working with the therapist has made me a better pastor. And certainly I am a more loving, caring father to Evan.

WORDS FROM JEENIE

Many times I have filled out forms for child abuse. I've looked at bruises, neck chokes, and lash marks with another professional present. However, the emotional scars are invisible.

Person after person has sat in my office with enormous pain over the ill treatment suffered due to a parent or spouse. Whether physical or sexual, it is always emotional. It practically tears their hearts out.

Seldom does a client need to let me know they have been abused. The signs are there. Even when they do not bring it up until months later, I base my therapy on the fact they have been abused. Sometimes they say, "You knew all along."

My heart has also gone out to parents who are the abusers, as is the case in this pastoral story. Most often they also lived through abuse as a child. Parent after parent has been overcome with grief, remorse, and horror as their admission came forth.

When I report, I always inform the perpetrator and, if possible, call in the abuse during our session. I want everything to be above board. In my state, I inform the patient that for the first offense, Child Protective Services will be at their door. They will take a good look around the home to check for unsanitary living conditions. If it appears to be filthy, the kitchen cupboards and refrigerator will be checked to see if there is sufficient food. Generally, when the house looks in normal order, the case is noted but nothing more ensues.

As with the pastor's son, the child is always interviewed alone—usually at school. They want to ensure the parent will have no impact on the child telling the truth.

Abuse is often generational, passed down from generation to generation. I inform my clients, "The chain of abuse must be broken, and since you are the one in therapy, you must break the shackle."

There is hope for both those who perpetrate and those who are victimized, when they work on the root issues with honesty in ongoing, deep therapy.

Unfortunately, the emotional scars remain.

THEN CAME THE ECHO
CHARLES R. BROWN

On the edge of life's canyon
I freely shouted my pain.
Life isn't fair!—isn't fair—isn't fair.
I deserve better!—better—better—better.
Nobody loves me!—*I do—I do—I do.*

Speech suddenly stolen
It seemed like a Zechariah moment.
Not sure, I yelled,
Who's there?—*I AM—I AM—I AM!*
Hands trembling
My knees buckled
until my face was on the ground.

Then came the echo
without a word from my
complaining lips.
I love you—I love you—love you—love you.
Still I could not move.
Unbelief was pounding in my chest.

I know your pain.
Come hang with me.
See what I saw from my Father's view.
I was separated from Him,
so you would never be.

Lifted up, body and soul,
my heartbeat transformed
from uncertainty to a childlike trust.

Thank You, Savior!
You're welcome, my child—my child—my child.

The first step to getting out of an abusive situation is to recognize the danger and to cry out for help as Emily did in the following story.

TRAUMATIZED
DR. MARY M. SIMMS

"I need help. Can you please help me? I don't have anyone to talk to."

This plea for help from a stranger on the other end of the line took me by surprise. I knew I was dealing with a possible crisis. "Yes," I answered, "I would like to assist you, but first let me get some more information so I can determine if I am the right person to help."

"I was referred by a major Christian organization, and they said you could help me. Please help me," the voice emphatically pleaded.

As the conversation continued, I realized the person on the other end of the telephone was in deep emotional pain and needed my help. As God's timing is always amazing, I just happened to have a same-day cancellation and could slot this person in. "Can you come to my office at 3:00 P.M.? I'd like to talk to you in person."

Emily arrived promptly for her appointment. After taking her personal history, I discovered she was 24 years old. She came from a physically and emotionally abusive background, which seemed to set her up for attracting unhealthy relationships where she was physically and emotionally abused as well. I surmised she was suffering from severe anxiety and depression. This was manifested by her inability to sleep and having constant thoughts of shame and guilt.

She said, "I'm embarrassed, and I feel as though I am such a terrible person."

"So, what did you do that was terrible?" I asked.

"I know I should never have married. Even when I prayed about it, I felt the Lord telling me to wait. I just couldn't see what was in front of me. I convinced my husband to marry me two years ago. At first everything was really great, but then when I wanted to go out with my friends, it started."

"What started?"

"The threatening, yelling, screaming, and hitting."

"Go on," I suggested.

"It felt like I was right back in my parents' home again. I got married to get away from the abuse, and now I find myself right back in it! I want to leave my husband, but my mom tells me to hang in there. She tells me that at least I have someone willing to work and pay the bills. She thinks things will get better."

"Yelling and screaming is one thing, but hitting is quite another. How often are you being hit physically?" I asked.

She paused for a moment, reluctant to share the information. "It happens at least once a week," she responded softly.

After assessing her safety, it appeared she could be in danger of getting hurt or of hurting her abuser. When she got hit, she defended herself by hitting back.

"Once the police came, and I was afraid I would be arrested because my husband had scratches on his arms and face. But he fled the scene, so I was not arrested."

Emily tended to minimize and normalize what happened because this was an all too common occurrence that she witnessed when she was a little girl. She reported that she watched her dad physically abuse her mom from the age of 2 until the time when she moved out of the family home at about age 16. Although she never saw her mom defend herself, Emily thought she was doing much better because she at least tried to defend herself.

"Do you think things will get better?" I asked

Well, uh, I don't know, but I guess since I did not listen to the Lord or anyone about waiting to get married, I should try and stick it out!"

"Is your mom still going through the abuse with your dad?" I asked.

"Yes, but now he just talks down to her. He is sick and can't hit her anymore. She is his caregiver. She seems resentful now because she doesn't do much for herself except take care of him."

"Do you see that same cycle repeating in your situation?"

"Yes, but I don't know what to do! As my mom said, 'I made my bed, so now I have to lie in it.'"

This cycle of guilt and shame often perpetuated by the abuser keeps a victim locked into this kind of thinking and puts her in danger of being hurt or even killed by her abuser. Growing up in an abusive environment shapes the feelings of unworthiness, and often these distorted beliefs are modeled and supported by family members who have lived this way as well.

Emily had a lot of recovery work to do. First, she had to acknowledge her own anger issues with her dad for violating her mom, herself, and her siblings. She needed to see how her anger, beliefs, and unworthiness created vulnerabilities in her own life that were often exploited.

Also, she had to deal with her anger toward her mom for staying in a situation that endangered her and her siblings.

Finally, Emily needed to find a healthy church environment where she was taught the love, grace, and mercy of God, a God who could forge a path for her as it was originally purposed to be.

As she started understanding God's love for her and her value and worth in Him, she could slowly make positive decisions to move away from the abuse.

⁓ WORDS FROM JEENIE ⁓

An abuser who will control, manipulate, and perpetuate abuse has an antenna that seeks out vulnerabilities in prospective partners that they can exploit.

Sometimes, people who abuse have been abused themselves in childhood—physically, emotionally, or sexually. A child is helpless in the care and presence of an adult and is totally dependent for food, shelter, clothes, and emotional love and support. Therefore, if the child is abused, he or she is stuck with nowhere to turn and no way out. So, the child learns various coping mechanisms to live in the abusive home.

The young woman in the story desperately wanted to get out of a dysfunctional home, which may have affected her decision to marry quickly. Since her mother also suffered abuse in her relationship, her mother was unable to provide the kind of wisdom and support so desperately needed by her daughter. Without appropriate intervention and supportive services, the dynamics of unhealthy relationships may be perpetuated through family generations.

Thankfully, the young woman in the story received professional help and began to value herself and make healthy choices about her relationship. With assistance and support, she was breaking the cycle and becoming strong enough to move away from the situation.

DETECTIVE TOM'S TIP:
STATISTICS:

Our police department has about 360 domestic violence cases a year, but only 20 or less result in shooting or stabbing—less than 10 percent of the cases. However, these violent crimes take place in seconds or minutes and often result in the victim being killed. There is not usually a period of contemplation.

God works in mysterious ways. Just when Diana didn't see any way out of her difficult life, God opened the door for her to escape through an "angel" at the police station.

FROM THE DEPTHS OF THE ABYSS
DIANA LEAGH MATTHEWS

"What is this?" Duncan demanded, holding up my notes.

"That is the information for my job interview."

"I told you not to take that job!" he said.

"Why not?" The job was 15 minutes away, and I'd already been told the job was mine.

"It's too far away," he said.

I stared at this man in disbelief. After three years together I felt he was more of a stranger than a husband. "I worked near there before. That's not too far for me to drive," I reminded him.

"I don't care. You won't take the job. You had the offer at the gas station. Take that."

I was sick. In three years I'd gone from being a successful travel agent to pumping gas. "Why can't I drive?" We had four cars and just the two of us driving, except when his sister, Marian, decided to use one.

"My enemies have a hit on you," he explained. He'd used this line so much I didn't believe him anymore. He refused to pay my bills, so the car I had before we met had been repossessed. Driving me everywhere was his way of controlling me.

"I don't care. I'll take my chances," I called his bluff. He pulled me across the room by my hair and pushed me onto the floor.

"Clean that," he demanded. Hiding my tears, I was soon on my hands and knees scrubbing the floor. I felt like Cinderella when she was with her wicked stepmother.

"What have you done now?" Marian asked when she came over. I didn't answer, but continued with my cleaning.

"Well?" she demanded. I finally explained our conversation.

"You're so silly," she sneered.

I wanted to scream. "I'm tired of you and Duncan trying to control me."

"We're only looking out for you," Marian cooed. "We love you, but no one else does."

"If this is love, then I'd rather be alone," I retorted as I stormed out of the house. I needed to put some space between us and cool down.

When I returned home Duncan yelled, "I should kill you now!" He twisted my arm and pushed me onto the floor. "This isn't over," he promised.

The next morning, after I'd been cleaning house for three hours, I went into the computer room to check on a few job inquiries.

"Why are you on the computer?" he demanded less than 15 minutes later.

"I was checking for responses to my job search," I explained.

"I told you to take the job at the gas station."

Being around this man who I had a love/hate relationship with made me physically ill at times. I felt defeated on my way to take a shower. This was not the man I first met and fell in love with. This monster was nothing like that man, but I had nowhere to turn. He'd cut off all communication with friends and family when we married. The only person I could turn to was God. I talked to Him more than anyone these days, but sometimes I wondered if He heard me.

"How do I get out of this mess, God?"

I discovered Duncan had taken my computer away while I was in the shower. "Why?" I asked, but he gave no answer. I was so angry that I called the police. I'd previously worked with some officers who told me to document everything.

With the police in the hall with me, Duncan took the time to pull the hard drive and memory out before returning the computer. I couldn't believe his gall. When I asked him why, his response was, "My nephew needs to fix the system."

Later that day when he left, I walked the five blocks to his nephew's house. The young man looked at me strangely when I asked for my hard drive. When Duncan found out what I had done, he choked me and then pushed me to the ground.

We were past making amends. I hid the fact that I'd made contact with my family and planned to leave when he was out of town the next month.

Five days later Christmas arrived. "Merry Christmas, darling," he greeted me with a kiss. I was surprised. "Let bygones be bygones" he said.

I hoped things had improved. Marian and her husband, Colin, arrived. Colin dealt with the family drama by driving a truck cross-country and seldom came home.

The civility was short-lived, and the next morning I was greeted with a slap to the face. The final showdown came two days after Christmas.

Duncan refused to pick me up from my new job at the gas station. I had to walk the six miles home. When I arrived home, he was at his nephew's. Less than an hour later, he called and demanded I bring a few plastic bags to him.

When I arrived, he continued to put me down. "You're not worth anything. No one will ever want you."

"You can manipulate Marian and Colin, but I'm tired of it," I screamed, storming out of his nephew's house. With nowhere else to go, I returned home. Duncan arrived moments later and continued to taunt me.

For years he'd been throwing various affairs in my face. When he made a vulgar remark, I slapped him for the first time.

"You can't leave," Marian begged, entering the room. "If you do, they'll kill you." This threat did not have a hold on me anymore.

I snapped and put my hands around her throat. "Maybe they'll kill you instead," I said before letting go. Duncan stormed out of the room and called the police.

"I don't understand why she gets so worked up," he told the officers. Then he turned to me and referred to me as "honey." I was disgusted by the act he and Marian put on for the officers, who had made numerous visits in the last year.

Charges were pressed, and I was taken downtown and processed. Fortunately, an angel on duty allowed me to call Mom. The New Year was staring us in the face, and I had to wait until after the holiday to appear before a judge. I spent those days crying, praying, and struggling to make sense of everything.

This was an answer to prayer, however, and I knew I'd not return to Duncan. On the other hand, my heart was breaking. This was the man I loved and vowed to spend my life with.

The next Friday I went before a judge and received probation and time served. I went home with Mom. I was blessed to have an understanding family, who gave me space to grieve and heal. I began counseling with a professional trained in domestic abuse. I attended church with Mom and got involved with Divorce Care and Celebrate Recovery.

Duncan had no idea where I was, but tried to continue controlling me through email. I didn't respond, nor did I leave a forwarding address. I opened a post office box and let my creditors know my new address. I also began using a prepaid phone. I changed my email address and passwords.

I found a job that did not have a lot of stress and continued in-depth counseling for more than two years. Writing was my best therapy. I journaled my feelings—good and bad. I began a daily Bible study and prayertime.

The best thing I did was to forgive Duncan and Marian. This wasn't easy, but each day I made a conscious effort to say, "I forgive them." The more I did this, the easier it became, and the better I felt. I soon saw a change within myself.

My healing took close to four years before I realized I was moving forward. I did a lot of soul searching and sought God's will for my life. Now I ask God to shower His love on me. Each day is a move toward a better, God-filled life.

❧ WORDS FROM JEENIE ❧

Controllers manipulate, are habitual and prolific liars, and often abuse. They have no problem with a bold-faced fabrication and can come up with a seemingly valid one in a split second, as they have had much practice. Duncan went to great lengths to control every event of Diana's life, including preventing her from driving and from obtaining a job that she wanted and would help her to feel good about herself and gain independence. She describes being "choked"—which is actually strangulation—a deadly and very common tactic of physical violence that is a high-risk indicator of lethality for the victim. The statement that "his enemies had a hit on her" were simply the abuser's veiled threats to take her life.

While it seems so unfair that the police believed Duncan and his sister when charges were pressed against the true victim, this scenario is replayed day after day in police jurisdictions across the nation. Abusers not only manipulate their victims, they often use male privilege and their masculinity to engage and manipulate law enforcement as well. In Diana's case, she was put on probation, which may have been her first step. It reminds me of Joseph when he did the right things in the sight of God, yet was sent to prison because Potiphar believed his wife's lie. Even so, God took care of him in that dark and filthy prison and in time put him second in command on the throne of Egypt (see Genesis 39–47).

Eventually, Diana was released from her prison of victimization and came into a life of wholeness and peace. God blessed her because she was willing to forgive and start over, just as Joseph did.

Forgiveness sets us free.

> [Forgiving] is going to be hard for many abuse victims—it will take time and God's help. You need to come to a point where you can forgive your abuser. . . .
>
> Forgiving is not saying that what your abuser did to you is all right. Forgiving is to release your emotional desire to retaliate against your offender for what he did to you. You let go of those feelings of hatred and revenge. Forgiving means you are willing to let God and/or the authorities deal with the offender. Forgiveness

does not mean that you try to remove the natural consequences that should follow any act of sinful abuse. . . .

Forgiveness is a choice we make to extend "grace" to another through God's Holy Spirit.

—DETECTIVE SERGEANT DONALD STEWART, *REFUGE*

REFLECTION: I need to find the strength to forgive my abuser and move on with my life.

PRAYER: *Lord, help me to learn to forgive. And teach me to embrace the truth that I am created in Your image, that my life has purpose, and that I am precious in Your sight. In Jesus' name I pray, amen.*

CHAPTER 10

The Chains Fall Off

You, dear children, are from God and have overcome
them, because the one who is in you is greater than
the one who is in the world.

—1 JOHN 4:4

JOHN NEWTON PENNED the following words to his famous song, "Amazing Grace," while sitting in a tiny shed in a beautiful garden in Olney, England. At the time he was an ordained minister, serving at the Olney Church nearby.

Thro' many dangers, toils, and snares,
I have already come;
'Tis grace hath bro't me safe thus far,
And grace will lead me home.

Previously, John had been a master of slave-trading ships and had nightmares over the ill treatment, abuse, and deaths of so many slaves. Then on a homeward voyage, while he was attempting to steer the ship through a violent storm, he exclaimed, "Lord, have mercy upon us." Later in his cabin he reflected on those words and believed God had guided him through the storm. He knew the chains of his past had fallen off, and God had forgiven him and granted him grace.

In 1780, Newton left Olney to become rector of St. Mary Woolchurch in London. There he met William Wilberforce and, although Newton was going blind, he aided and encouraged Wilberforce in the campaign for the abolition of slavery.

Chris Tomlin added lyrics to "Amazing Grace" that speak of the chains falling off and the person being set free. And just as Newton weathered the storm and was set free of his past through grace, those who are living in abusive situations can also weather life's storms, have their chains fall off, and be set free of that life. By God's grace, they can start anew.

> *For it is by grace you have been saved, through faith—and this is not from yourselves, it is the gift of God—not by works, so that no one can boast* (Ephesians 2:8–9).

Like many girls, Terri had marriage on the mind when she went to college. When Carl asked her to marry him, she thought he was the answer to all her dreams and prayers. Little did she know that her dreams would soon turn into nightmares.

ACCEPTABLE ABUSE
TERRI MARTIN

As a young girl, marriage was on my mind, as were babies, a house with a white picket fence, and living happily ever after. Isn't that the dream of most girls?

My turn came while in a Christian college. I wasn't especially attracted to the young man, but I dated him anyway. However, I grew to love Carl, and in a short time he asked for my hand in marriage. I felt happy that someone wanted me.

Growing up in a poor, divorced home, I looked forward to something better in my adult life. In my opinion, our family was not respected, especially in our church. It boiled down to the fact we had little materially, and I believed we were thought of as dirty and stupid. None of which was true. Over the years, my self-esteem was quite damaged, and I did not see myself as an equal with my peers.

So, for marriage, I took the first person who came along. There was no money for a wedding, even though my uncle, a pastor, offered his church and help. Carl refused. At his insistence, we traveled to a nearby state to marry, accompanied by his sister. I got up my courage and requested a pastor marry us. At the county seat, they gave us a name of a pastor who would assist us. He was a kind, gracious man, but the ceremony was over in about five minutes.

Of course, we had no honeymoon. Upon arriving back in our city, my husband suggested a rundown motel for our first night. I was deeply disappointed.

Returning to college, girlfriends asked to see my ring. Embarrassed, I showed them a simple gold band and explained we had matching rings. Their comments were less than enthusiastic.

Thus began a life of almost absolute control by my husband. I left college for a full-time job so Carl could complete his degree. I didn't return for nearly 15 years to earn my BA.

Carl could be extremely outgoing to others when it served his purpose. Most of the time, however, he kept a tight rein over me. Thinking this was my obligation as a wife, I concurred.

We were involved in church. However, we would often arrive early and wait in the car to enter just before the service began. On those Sundays, he would then escort me and our daughter out the side door in order for us not to have any social interaction.

Vividly I recall being allowed to go on only one outing with girlfriends to a Tupperware party. Upon arriving home early afternoon, Carl stood in the middle of the street, tapping his watch because I arrived two minutes late. Then began the silent treatment, which was often used as my punishment. Sometimes it lasted a few hours, other times as long as two weeks. Consequently, I tried desperately to please him.

My social life was practically nonexistent. He read every letter I wrote or received from former college girlfriends and scrutinized my telephone calls. All were met with great disapproval and shaming. Since my self-worth was low, I succumbed.

To make a long story short, I received a telephone call one Sunday afternoon while Carl was playing tennis. A woman told me the sordid story of her affair with my husband and her current pregnancy. Carl told her to get rid of it, even though she was also married. The woman confirmed many other affairs my husband had in different schools where he had been a principal.

Struck with terror, I confronted my husband, who would admit nothing. The next morning, I called my alma mater to enroll and complete the last year of my degree. I graduated in May. I then began a master's degree, realizing I would need to support myself and my daughter in a profession. I was propelled by the verse in Proverbs 16:9: *In his heart, a man plans his course, but the Lord determines his steps.* As I walked, God led.

The night my husband walked out, the emotional tearing held a stranglehold on my feelings, wrapped rigidly around my body, and permeated my thoughts. Even though my being was enveloped with suffering, there was a sense that God had removed him, for I was incapable of ending the marriage on my own. It seemed as though God had closed the door and, in awe of a holy God, I could not reopen it. Although I experienced several years of loneliness and pain, I never asked my husband to return. Nor did he ask.

God has done amazing things in my life. I earned two master's degrees, taught in high schools, and became a school administrator. I have spoken internationally and on radio and TV and have written ten books. I am truly humbled and grateful for God's guidance and intervention. As time has elapsed, I am no longer steeped in low self-worth. Nor do I allow anyone to control or abuse me. I am set free.

WORDS FROM JEENIE

As a therapist, I know that one of the key elements in abuse is isolation. Keep the victim away from family, friends, and neighbors. Monitor with tight controls. Even though her experience does not indicate physical abuse, *control is abuse*. It is covert (underground) and not easily detected.

So many women, and sometimes men, in my therapy office express shock when I uncover the fact they have actually been abused. Most people state, "I just thought I needed to try to do better, but it never worked."

I think of a pole-vaulter who, at the beginning of his sport, sets the bar at a low height level. It is one he knows he can eventually reach, but it will take practice and effort. After much struggle and endurance, he reaches the goal and raises the bar. The vaulter continues to persevere, and after each success, raises the bar until he ultimately reaches heights of which he had only dreamed.

In an abusive setting, the controller sets the "bar"—the standard of expectation. The victim strives and works to attain and please, and just as he or she is almost there, the abuser raises the bar. No matter how hard he or she tries, it is never enough. The victim repeatedly falls short. The controller wins—again.

DETECTIVE TOM'S TIP:
ADVICE TO THOSE AWARE OF THE ABUSE:

Too many friends and family members remain silent. Police and other experts want them to come forward. They need to report the abuse they are aware of even though it happens behind closed doors. They can do something rather than stand by and do nothing. They can call the police department or domestic violence hotlines and say something like, "What can I do to get my sister out of this abusive relationship?" Just because it happens behind closed doors does not mean it should not be exposed to the sunshine.

A father takes out on his teenage daughter his enormous grief over losing his wife. Only by understanding and forgiving him is A. G. able to break free and have her chains fall off.

HOPE FOR HIDDEN SCARS
A. G. COOMBS

I always wondered if he could hear me breathing as I hid in my bedroom closet—or did he just innately know I was there. Through the slits of the wooden twin doors I watched, waiting for his form to fill the white square of light that appeared when my bedroom door was torn open violently. Most of the time I could hear him before he arrived: the front door smashing into its abused frame, a bottle crashing against an innocent wall. He always came. And I never let myself believe that he wouldn't, not even for a second. For I found that it was easier to prepare for pain than to pretend it wasn't there—wasn't coming.

Life wasn't always like this, though. Yet when my mother passed away from ovarian cancer when I was 16, in the summer of 2003, my father passed away, too, from the man he once was. He replaced the lips of his wife with the lips of a bottle, replaced the warmth of her fingers laced into his with the warmth of cigarettes woven in between two of his. He was a man destroyed, defeated.

Yet I never blamed him for his grief and, as strange as this may sound, I never hated him for hitting me. I would bleed. I would shriek. I would cry. Sometimes I would be beaten unconscious. But in the mornings, or whatever hour I awoke, I could hear him in his room, behind his locked door, weeping before what I imagined was the one picture of my mother he kept in the house.

How could I hate someone I understood more than anyone else? Is it not true that pain penetrates the boundaries of what is incommunicable and therefore unites one another? How could I vacate his presence from my heart when he was the only parent I had left, and I the only child he had and would ever have?

Questions and doubts swept over me like a wind, erasing every boundary I believed in. Lines of decency may be drawn into the sands of society, but what occurs in one's home, regardless if it is or isn't a matter of sobriety, is something personal, something no one else quite understands, and in consequence, is something one feels the need to handle quietly.

Makeup can cover bruises. Red lipstick removes little tears in lips. Yet scars are souvenirs, even if they're only visible in certain instances of light. And it is the scars we do not see in one another, the hidden ones, the ones of the heart that hurt the most, even if they are only visible in the darkest hours of night. When we are alone, uncomforted by the drone of a clock, we realize that things may continue to be this way, and all we have is hope—hope that somehow, someway, things will change.

The change in my own life came unexpectedly. I was in a grocery store, of all places, standing silently in line when a little boy, no taller than my knee, came up to me, tugged at my shirt, and waved his hand to signal a whisper. As I bent down, he told me he loved me. I was informed later that those were the only words he spoke besides *Dad*, *dog*, and *Mom*, but at the time it moved my emotions unexplainably. I ran out of the store crying.

The boy's older brother, whom I did not see in line, came out and found me folded over, face in my hands, sitting at a bench not far from the entrance. I was crying hysterically. I hadn't heard those words since my mother had passed. The boy's brother sat down beside me and comforted me, not by touch, but by prayer. He sat there, folded over, with his hands clasped together, praying out loud for me, someone he had never met.

I dried my eyes and thanked him. We exchanged numbers and our relationship grew. He invited me to church, where I met people who sought not to judge or condemn, but only wanted to listen and understand. I even dated the boy's brother for a time. Although our relationship didn't last, the relationship he introduced me to, my true Father, did and always will last.

I write this now, eight years after my mother passed, three years after I found my true Father, God, two years after I established my own residence, and one year after I finished my bachelor's degree in child psychology. And I can tell you, wholeheartedly, there is such a thing as change, such a thing as hope. No matter how impossible the two may seem—they exist. Today I talk to my birth father once or twice a year. He hasn't changed much, but neither has my love for him. The concept I began to create early in youth is still valid today. I love the person of my father, I pray for the person of my father, but I do not love or wish upon anyone else the actions of my father. Some scars may still remain, but I no longer feel their pain. I feel only peace.

My message to those who may be going through similar experiences is: Life is temporary. Just as my story is coming to an end, so will your circumstances come to end one day. And with every end, there is a new beginning.

⁓ WORDS FROM JEENIE ⁓

Walking on eggshells is often a daily occurrence in an abusive home. It also entails waiting for the other shoe to drop, because it always does. A. G. learned early it was much better to be prepared than to face the unexpected. Even when it appeared she was prepared, it actually was not the case since she never was quite sure what form the abuse would take until it was upon her. So, she constantly lived in a state of uncertainty. It appeared her father was taking out his enormous grief over the loss of his beloved wife on A. G.

A. G. has been willing to call the behavior of her father what it was—abuse. That is the pathway to healing and eventual forgiveness. Even so, she has put a healthy boundary between them, knowing once or twice yearly is enough connection.

Thankfully, God used the young man in the parking lot to be bold enough to care for A. G. and pray with her. He lifted her up, introducing her to the Father who would never leave.

The power of verbal prayer for another has great impact. As God has led me in counseling, I have prayed aloud for many people. I've seen the enormous impact the Spirit of God has on them, even those who do not know Christ. When someone says, "Pray for me," I usually grab their hand and pray immediately. Our heavenly Father is in the life-changing business, and we need to follow the whispers of the Holy Spirit and trust God for the outcome. We never know when a life will be changed as was A. G.'s.

> *Be joyful in hope, patient in affliction, faithful in prayer* (Romans 12:12).

Although Ashley was aware of the abuse that went on in her family, it was hard for her to see her mother move out and start a new life.

TEARDROPS FROM THE SOUL
ASHLEY HARRINGTON

I sat in my living room and looked out the window. The rain had stopped and rays of sunshine streamed through the clouds. The phone rang, and when I answered I heard Dad's voice, "Ashley, where's your mother?"

"I don't know." There was a long silence, and then he said, "Last night, I came home and everything is gone. I don't believe you don't know where she is."

Before I could reply, he hung up. I sat there a moment in a daze, feeling both sorrow and anger. My thoughts churned, *I feel sorry for you, Dad. Mom loves you. But she can't stand living with your out-of-control alcoholism anymore! My heart breaks for Mom.*

I picked up the phone and dialed Mom's new number. "Hello," her voice, sounded stronger.

"It's me, Mom. Dad just called and wanted to know where you are. He hung up on me when I wouldn't tell him." I heard a big sigh from her.

"I start my new job next week." She continued, "Thank you for your help in getting me moved and settled in. I hope our conversation didn't upset you too much."

"It did, but I asked the question. I'm OK. It's just sometimes the truth hurts."

"I'm sorry, Ashley. I love you. Hopefully, things will get better."

"I love you, too, Mom. Joe will be home soon so I need to get dinner started."

"Give the kids a hug from Grandma."

"I will."

I got up and went into the kitchen and started peeling potatoes for the stew. My mind wandered back to the previous day when we'd helped Mom and my brothers move.

All morning long Mom had shed tears. Finally, I got her to go out to lunch with me. When we came back to her apartment I asked, "Were you and Dad happy before his drinking got so bad?"

"For a while, but he already had a drinking problem, and I kept telling myself he would get better. The first year we were married we bought our first home. Then I got pregnant with you. Things got better for a while. But the day our friends had a baby shower for me, Dad went off with some buddies, and he came home drunk."

"Did you ever think of leaving him?"

"Yes, but I remembered how my mom struggled after my dad left."

"Did Dad even want me?" I asked.

"Yes, Ashley, he was really excited. But one night he came home drunk, and he became abusive."

"But you were expecting me."

"Yes, but he didn't know what he was doing. He was too drunk."

"What did he do?"

"He forced himself on me."

"You mean he raped you?"

"Yes, the next day I started having contractions, and I thought I'd lose you. When I confronted him with what he'd done, he broke down and cried. He cried tears from his soul. I believed he was sorry. Things improved after that. He didn't drink so much."

We sat there in silence for a while. My mind flashed back through the years. I realized that what Mom had just shared with me explained the fear I'd often seen in her eyes. She had experienced, within the first year of their marriage, how cruel Dad could be when drunk out of his mind.

"So, when did it get bad again?"

"After we bought our business, he didn't have to be accountable to anyone. He was his own boss. Often he'd nip at a bottle during the day." By the time Mom finished her story I was crying.

"Mommy, Mommy," my son's voice brought me back to the present. I looked over at him where he sat playing with his toy cars.

"Look what I made," he said proudly. He'd made a bridge between two chairs with a piece of cardboard.

"Lee, that's great. What a good job."

I went over and hugged him, and as I held my son I silently prayed. "Lord, please let me see Dad repent someday. Help Mom to put her life back together again. Help me to forgive."

In my heart I knew that God's plan in a marriage did not include abuse. More than anything I wanted peace for all of us. As I prayed, I felt my sorrowful heart being filled with peace—a peace beyond all understanding. I knew that God understood. I knew that my heavenly Father would never abandon us.

WORDS FROM JEENIE

Children, even as adults, do not want to choose between their parents, as they love them both. They are caught in the middle. Ashley was quite aware of the abuse in the home, yet her love for her father remained.

Even preverbal toddlers sense what is happening in their homes, producing inner turmoil. They are incapable of expressing their feelings, but they are cognizant of the chaos. Actually, no one in the home is capable of understanding or changing the scenario. Without professional intervention, often these emotions and beliefs are carried into adulthood.

Family members learn to cope with the abusive situations. It is all too familiar, and each person must choose how to respond. Each practices his or her specific coping mechanisms in order to survive.

In some cases, whatever type of abuse transpired in their home is repeated as an adult in their marital relationship. They learned how to cope in their childhood home, thus bringing the dysfunctional survival systems into adulthood. They previously ascertained what to expect and how to act accordingly.

Without professional help, the cycle will likely repeat itself—sometimes for generations. The chain of abuse must be broken.

REFLECTION: Do you believe that the truth will set you free?

PRAYER: *Lord, thank You for helping me face the truth. Guide me as I seek counseling. Help me to believe that Jesus Christ holds the keys to release me from the chains of abuse. In Jesus' name I pray, amen.*

CHAPTER 11

No Turning Back

O Lord my God, I called to you for help,
and you healed me.

—Psalm 30:2

FAITH IN THE Lord is a light in the darkness. When doubts question your ability to make the right decisions, faith whispers, *You are not alone.* In the midst of the storm when fear overcomes, faith whispers, *Lean not on your own understanding.* Like the reliable light from a lighthouse, faith guides you to safety. As you reach out for help, faith reminds you *to trust.* When the tears flow because you don't know who you are anymore, faith reassures, *You are God's child.*

When you've weathered the storm and have reached a safe harbor, faith whispers, *Rest.* Once again friends and family share your life without intimidation. You've learned to laugh again. Faith encourages you, *No turning back.*

> *Faith is the confidence that what we hope for will actually happen; it gives us assurance about things we cannot see* (Hebrews 11:1 NLT).

Although the past eight years have been challenging for Amy, she has weathered the storm and found a place where she and her children have peace in their home and with God.

A PEACEFUL PLACE
AMY MILLER

I'm looking for a new apartment, although I love the one we've lived in the past two years. The fact is, my kids and I have moved several times since their father, Ed, and I divorced. Each time I promise them, "We'll be fine," and they sacrifice a little more privacy and space so I can financially support the three of us on my church secretary's salary.

With my daughter in college and a son preparing to leave the nest in a couple of years, it feels right to downsize a bit. That will allow a little breathing room in the budget to enjoy buying a new pair of shoes or going out for a nice dinner once in a while.

The past 8 years have been more than challenging, but the kids and I agree that the peace we've gained is worth it. I spent nearly 20 years with their dad, none of them particularly happy. It was different before we married. He changed after the wedding and grew harder to live with after our first child was born.

Three years into our marriage I began to suspect he was seeing someone. I just didn't want to believe it. It wasn't until he got so confident he didn't even try to cover his trail that I gathered hard facts to confront him.

He promised he'd break it off, and he did, but 2 years later I discovered he was with someone new. I began to counsel with our pastor, clinging to the hope that we could somehow work through his indiscretions. I wanted so much for our children to be raised in a Christian home with both parents present.

It took a severe bout of depression, a diagnosis of a hyperthyroid condition, an additional diagnosis of adrenal fatigue, a peptic ulcer from stress, insomnia, and a myriad of other physical symptoms to convince me that the children and I were better off without him.

Ed's manipulation and lies were so prevalent the kids grew to mistrust every word he spoke. He rarely kept a promise, and when we vacationed, our son, Connor, frequently caught him staring at young girls in bikinis on the beach. It was no surprise when we discovered Ed's pornography addiction.

Years of feeling like I just wasn't enough led me to a dark place that I wasn't sure I'd ever return from, but when I saw the advertisement in the church bulletin, "Secretary Needed," I knew I had to apply.

I hadn't interviewed in years. I was still raising our children. But I summoned the courage and was hired, and that day my confidence soared from nothing to something measurable. That one small victory lifted my spirit to the point of feeling hopeful for the first time in years.

Ed was not happy that I got a job outside of our home, but I believe God led me to that position to prepare me for what lay ahead and to provide supportive, prayerful people to encourage and strengthen me through the fight.

Our divorce was more of an emotional battle for me than anything. My attorney ended up retiring in the middle of the case, handing me off to a young woman who was barely out of law school. Needless to say, I didn't get the best settlement, but it never seemed to matter. God has provided what we need—not everything we want—but definitely what we need.

The kids and I are content, and we laugh a lot at home—something we rarely did with Ed. We watch silly television shows and movies together, and the kids' faith is growing. We don't have extra money for expensive clothes and trips, but we have each other. Plus, we have peace in our home and lots of joy, and to us, that's a priceless gift.

Last year Ed stopped by the apartment to tell us he was moving several hundred miles away. I think he wanted the kids to beg him to stay, or at least say they would miss him, but they didn't.

"OK," was all they muttered before turning and walking back into our apartment. Part of me actually felt sad for him. I wonder if Ed will ever realize how incredibly empty his life is.

As for me, I get lonely once in a while, but God continually surprises me by bringing new opportunities and new friends into my life as the seasons go by. I am proud of the compassion and kindness I see my children display. And I'm feeling stronger than I have in years.

Last month's physical rendered me healthy (for my age) and whole. Unbelievable. I have never felt stronger, more blessed, and more content. Praise be to God!

⤖ WORDS FROM JEENIE ⤕

Amy's story is yet another one of hanging on through affairs, lies, broken promises, and an unhealthy marriage.

I am a firm believer in trying everything possible to keep the marriage, for that is God's best. However, it takes two. If one is unwilling to work, change, and grow, it can be a rather hopeless situation.

Vividly I recall sitting in a counseling office of an older godly man. It was our first session, and evidently he sensed my husband was not interested. He asked my husband a poignant question. "Are you willing to work on this marriage with no guarantee of success?"

Standing up and charging toward the door, my former spouse stated, "I'm not willing to work on it—period."

After he left, I told the counselor, "I can't accept that." To which he replied, "That's not the point, Jeenie. He will not work on it, and it looks like your marriage is over." Eventually, it was.

As Amy's children grew into teenagers, they began to see the truth of their father. Watching his actions and hearing the unfulfilled promises and lies, they began to distrust. This is not uncommon for adolescents. Some even encourage their mothers to obtain a divorce so they can have a family that is tranquil and sane.

Amy was brave enough to continue to raise her children on a limited church secretary income. They all had to tighten their belts and live in a rather small apartment. It appears her kids were cooperative and eager to help their mother make their home a good one. I'm sure they grew in love and respect for each other, learned the merits of hard work, and realized the value of a dollar, even though they were not able to have things others took for granted.

Colossians 3:15 states: *Let the peace of Christ rule in your hearts.* I like the fact that the verse started with the word "Let." God's peace is abundant, and all we need do is open up, consent, allow, and let it permeate our entire being.

Amy stated they finally found a peaceful existence and experienced God's tranquility in all its fullness. So can we.

Thanks to her sister's encouragement, Val began to realize what she thought was normal was actually abuse, and her husband's behavior was something she should not tolerate.

THE ESCAPE
V. C. WISDOM

"I wondered when you'd wake up and get away from that man, Val," my sister, Anne, said when I called to tell her I had filed for divorce. "He's abused you all these years."

"It isn't abuse. He's never hit me. He just yells at me and makes me feel like everything that goes wrong is my fault,"

I said. "He should be grateful I've paid all my car expenses plus life insurance for both of us all these years. Instead, he quit paying any bills. I pay for everything now, so I might as well be on my own."

Anne's next words seemed hard for me to believe. "Sometimes emotional abuse is worse than physical." Derogatory remarks were a part of my marriage for so long, I accepted them as normal. Although Stan spoke the robotic words, "I love you," his routine cursing and uncaring actions said the opposite.

I sought professional help to deal with my fears and nightmares. Yet my screams continued to pierce the night from a recurring dream of being stabbed. I prayed for strength, as during the day the verbal attacks intensified.

The turning point came one February. I had planned to attend a ladies prayer group, a rare solace because I worked a day job in addition to assisting my husband in his sales venture, a losing business. I waved at him puttering outside near his workshop as I hurried down the back steps to my car. "I'm going to a ladies prayer group. I'll be back about noon."

"You can't go. I need you to help me get ready for my next event," Stan said.

"I'll help you when I get back."

He spewed a diatribe of how I wanted his business to fail so he'd have to get a regular job. "I'm never going to work for anyone else again," he said. His voice escalated with accusations of my unwillingness to help him. He repeated his demands that I stay home. "You can go to church when I'm gone on my business trip," he said. "When I'm home, you have to ask if I need you before you go running off like there's nothing to do."

After initial disbelief, my anger—I like to think it was righteous indignation—surfaced. I screamed back, "I have to go to church. It's the only peace I have."

I had no peace that day nor during the weeks he was out of town. Dozens of his urgent phone calls demanded I put his needs first. While I stretched my food budget with meatless leftovers, he talked about eating seafood and steaks at favorite restaurants or cooking a special meal to treat other merchants during outdoor setups. My requests for money for household expenses were answered with, "I'm a little short this week." The answering machine spewed angry messages that reinforced his view of my failures such as: "You're never home when I need you" to "You should be home from work by now, not out running around."

I moved out one weekend while my husband was away. I didn't tell my pastor, friends, or next-door neighbors so they would be shielded from pressure to tell where I had gone. The next Sunday morning at church, I confided in an usher, a longtime friend, that he should keep an eye out for me because my husband might show up.

"You're just nervous," the usher said. "He's not like that." Shortly after the service began, my husband appeared at my pew. He gripped my arm and guided me out the side door of the sanctuary. The usher followed at a discreet pace. Later he said, "I wouldn't have believed that if I hadn't seen it with my own eyes."

I agreed to marriage counseling. At our first session, my husband began with, "Tell her what she's doing wrong so we can get this marriage back together." After a few weeks, guilt caused me to move back home. Nothing had changed. Demands and insults continued until I left my job, my home, and my friends and stepped into an unknown world branded with the big *D* of divorce.

Unable to afford an apartment, I lived with my sister for a year. I transitioned into a single room offered by a Christian woman who needed a live-in companion. Finally, I moved into an apartment of my own. I worked part-time, volunteered in the community and at a new church, and followed my long-suppressed dream of writing.

The nightmares ended. My life is pleasant. I'm an inspirational speaker and Bible teacher, but I've been silent about the verbal abuse that smothered those talents for a half century. Now, I've embarked on a new journey, a novel that will tell the most difficult scenes through the eyes of a fictionalized character. When her story is told, perhaps the invisible scars inflicted in my emotional prison will begin to heal.

⚜ WORDS FROM JEENIE ⚜

Abusers look good to the outside world, and they can keep up the charade indefinitely. Val sought protection from an usher at the church who was certain she did not need help because, "He's not like that." Only when he saw it for himself was he a believer. Val's sister was evidently the only person who called a spade a spade—naming the abuse.

Val's response was typical. "He has never hit me." That statement may be the primary reason women stay with abusers. They cannot believe verbal abuse is often more damaging and long lasting. Bruises heal and bones mend. Hearts, however, are left bleeding.

Another typical response was that Val took on the financial responsibility, plus helping her husband with a failing business. She tried to make things better for him, while her own needs were suppressed. An abuser often has a great sense of entitlement, as illustrated by his gourmet lifestyle when away from home and being short of cash when asked to help pay the bills. This story is a true picture of the antics of an abuser—

constant blaming, haranguing, accusing, interrogating, and unwillingness to think of anyone else's needs.

Unfortunately, few abusers change. By then, it is often too late for their marriage and family. Not only do they lose their wife, but often their children have seen so much they choose to no longer have a relationship with their father. Unless the abuser changes, and there is a commitment to Christ, and counseling, the situation is, indeed, very sad.

I've seen a multitude of women turn a corner and walk out—never to return. When enough is enough, seldom will a woman go back once the decision is thoughtfully made. And, almost without exception, they forge out a new and peaceful life for themselves.

Marge experienced a miracle in her marriage—a miracle that took a lot of work on both her husband's and her part.

THE RECONCILIATION
MARGE WINSTON

I screamed when my husband threw me down in the corral. I hit my head hard on the ground, but Stan kept banging my head into the dusty dirt. Then he grabbed me around the throat and started choking me.

This time he really is going to kill me! Fear gripped me as my mind raced. Scenes from our 30 years of marriage flashed before me. Memories filled my mind of Stan yelling at me, belittling me, and pushing me into walls when we were inside and dirt if we were outside.

And now his unrestrained anger is about to end my life, just as I had feared it would, I thought.

The next thing I knew, there was a female police officer holding smelling salts to my nose as my blurred vision began to clear.

"What happened?" I asked. Apparently I had blacked out, and the police had somehow made it out to our ranch in time to save me.

"How did you get here?" I asked the officer.

"Your daughter called 911. I can see the bruises on your neck where your husband tried to choke you." Looking more closely she asked, "Are you feeling OK?"

I nodded my head. Carol had learned about domestic violence in a recent college course. When she heard my screams, she decided enough was enough, and she called the police.

As my vision became clearer, I saw Stan across the way with handcuffs on. This scared me.

How much more will he punish me when this is over? I thought.

The policewoman explained the law to me. In our state, if police are called for a domestic violence case and there is evidence of abuse, the perpetrator is arrested. They did not ask me whether I wanted him taken away or would press charges. Scared as I was for my life, I would never have asked the police to take Stan away, because I knew his abuse would be even worse when he came back.

How embarrassing this is for him, I thought fearfully. Stan is a respected businessman in our midsize town. I watched in disbelief as the officers put Stan into the police car and drove away.

The policewoman explained, "Stan will be held in jail for 72 hours. Then he will be required to attend group therapy for domestic violence. And you both will be required to go to couples therapy. A mandatory restraining order has been placed on him. Stan will not be allowed to come onto your property."

"Wow," I mused, "Stan would never have agreed to this on his own."

Those were difficult days. I called my sister right after they took Stan away.

"I wonder what will happen next?" I asked, more to myself.

"I think you should leave Stan and get a divorce," Jane replied emphatically.

"Though I have not worked for many years, I do have the education and job skills to potentially support myself. My girls are grown now so I am free to work full-time."

"That's what you should do, Marge."

I was tempted to follow my sister's advice. I even paid a retainer fee to an attorney. But then I thought, *Stan makes good money. Do I want to leave all this wealth? I enjoy living on the ranch. And despite all this, I still love Stan. What should I do?*

When Stan was released from jail, he stayed with friends while I stayed at the ranch. After Stan had attended group therapy sessions, the restraining order was lifted. Then Stan stayed for several months in the apartment above our barn. I was OK with him being on the ranch, but I was not ready for him to be in the house with me.

Meanwhile, during this same time frame, my God-fearing mother died. Seeing her ebb away made me think about what's important in life . . . my relationship to God. I had walked away from God. Now I could see that I had made a mess of my life. My marriage was in shambles. Both Stan and I had had affairs and carried deep mistrust of one another. We each maintained a huge backlog of unresolved hurt from the relationship.

I came back to God saying, "OK, God, I have ruined my life, trying to do things my way. I am giving myself to You. Forgive me. Guide me in the next steps."

After this, I found I had a great hunger to learn more about God. I read the Bible and attended a women's Bible study. I began to change as I realized God's deep love for me. God began to heal me from my many psychological wounds, including my guilt and shame, both for what had been done to me and for what I had done. As Stan and I attended therapy together and I kept praying about it, I felt a desire to try one more time to make the marriage work. Despite all the pain, I still loved Stan.

Gradually our relationship began to heal. Stan no longer flared at me in anger. He quit calling me names. Through therapy he began to embrace his own pain of having been physically and sexually abused as a kid. I was able to be supportive of him. During therapy we had to work through the resentment, betrayal, and anger we felt toward each other. The process was painful and humbling. Gradually our hurts and suspiciousness were replaced by fledgling trust, and eventually love was reignited.

Soon Stan began attending church with me. And a year or so after that, he too dedicated his life to God. I never would have believed we could have found this much healing after so many years of hurt. I feel loved and finally at peace with myself, with God, and with Stan.

⚜ WORDS FROM JEENIE ⚜

It seems that Marge's marriage was destined to be doomed after 30 years of verbal and physical abuse, as well as both of them having had affairs. Whenever there is an affair, trust is gone. Though it can be built back with much work, counseling, and forgiveness, seldom does it ever become a total trusting marriage again. However, a marriage can still be good and solid even if there remains a small amount of distrust.

Marge, as many other victims, feared contacting law enforcement out of fear that the abuse would be worse when Stan was released. Even after Stan's arrest, she stated, "I never could have asked the police to take him away." In this case, the arrest and court intervention may have been a wake-up call for Stan.

While court-mandated domestic violence classes are the typical response in many states, just about every therapist I know dislikes court-appointed therapy. In the cases I've counseled, the client sat with arms crossed, a scowl across the countenance, and was unwilling to converse. Most of the communication I've received from them are grunts, shoulder shrugs, and "Yep" or "Nope." They put in their time and want me, as therapist, to sign their paperwork. My comments on the forms generally state, "The client attended six sessions." They put in their time, but seldom change.

Evidently Stan was not one of the typical court referrals and chose to work on his domestic violence issues, as well as participate in marital counseling. It is a rarity because there is a massive amount of work needed to produce lasting change.

I would imagine most people would consider the ending of this story to be a miracle. I definitely believe in miracles, but I also believe God gave us a will and brains to work on our own issues. When we do, He is there to help us get through the process. Many people want to be zapped with a miracle so they do not have to do the hard work.

As is often the case with a controller and abuser, they have been physically, sexually, and/or emotionally abused in childhood. Men tend to have a much more difficult time dealing with sexual abuse in childhood, believing somehow they could have stopped it. Healing begins to emerge when he realizes that as a youngster he was incapable of either standing up to or stopping an adult. My guess is that Stan dealt with those issues.

Couples who work on a marriage have the opportunity for a more healthy relationship. Those who don't—won't. I applaud both Stan and Marge for their willingness to change and grow. They also committed their lives to Christ, a chance for a brighter future.

John 14: 6–7 states:

> *Jesus answered, "I am the way and the truth and the life. No one comes to the Father except through me. If you really know me, you will know my Father as well."*

REFLECTION: God has led you to this point because He wants to have a personal, intimate relationship with you through His Son, Jesus Christ. We do not need to try to clean up or change our lives before coming to Christ. He welcomes us just as we are. Please pray the following prayer right now. If you already have a personal relationship with Jesus Christ, take this opportunity to recommit your life to Christ.

PRAYER: *Jesus, I'm hurting and want to have a personal relationship with You. I ask that You forgive me for all my sin and cleanse me. Please come into my life and be my Lord and Savior. I surrender to You and ask You to guide and protect me through the difficult days ahead. Please bestow on me the peace that only You can give. In Jesus' name I pray, amen.*

CHAPTER 12

Free to Live Again

For you created my inmost being;
you knit me together in my mother's womb.
I praise you because I am fearfully and
wonderfully made;
your works are wonderful,
I know that full well.

—Psalm 139:13–14

WHEN SUSAN'S BOYS were young, they found a caterpillar crawling around in the front yard. "Can we keep him?" asked Mike. "He will turn into a butterfly, won't he, Mom?"

Susan saw this as a wonderful teaching moment, so she said, "Let's find a jar to put him in." Richard ran into the garage, found the perfect jar, and poked holes in it. Mike gathered some grass and leaves and put those in the bottom. Then they carefully put the caterpillar inside.

To the boys' amazement, a few days later the caterpillar spun a cocoon. Susan put the jar on the shelf in the kitchen where the boys could watch it every day—and every day they did. About a month later, Richard exclaimed, "Look, Mom! He's turning into a butterfly."

Susan and the boys took the jar out to the front steps, set it down, and took the lid off. Soon a butterfly emerged from the cocoon, tested its wings, and eventually flew away.

If you have been in an abusive situation and felt like you were locked in a cocoon, now is your chance to get out and try your wings. It's time to become a butterfly and get on with your life. Each day will bring a new opportunity to attend classes, find a new job, renew friendships, and/or embrace a closer relationship with the Lord.

> *But those who hope in the Lord*
> *will renew their strength.*
> *They will soar on wings like eagles;*
> *they will run and not grow weary,*
> *they will walk and not be faint* (Isaiah 40:31).

Through a serious childhood illness, an abusive marriage, and an injury during the Olympics—Madeline never gave up.

NEVER GIVE UP
MADELINE MANNING MIMS

I should've seen the red flag when we were on the way to the courthouse to get married. We got in a big argument and he slapped me. I thought, *Maybe we shouldn't get married. I'm only 22.* But I was not one to give up easily.

Afterwards he said, "I'm sorry. I really feel bad about what happened."

I thought, *I know he is insecure. He just needs to know I'm his. Marrying him is the right thing to do.*

We went ahead with the ceremony. Then at a nearby hotel that night, he looked at me with a wild look in his eyes and said, "I've got you now! You'll never need to be around your friends and family members anymore."

I knew I'd messed up, and I was afraid of him. Unfortunately, things got worse from that day forward. I never knew whether a happy man would come home or a very angry one. On a bad day, he would jerk me around, shake me, and a couple of times he even choked me—but he never hit me again. I was thankful for that because he had been a football player, and he could've easily killed me.

When our son, John, was born, I thought things would change, but they did not. The situation only grew worse. I was brought up not to believe in divorce, and I didn't want to be a statistic, so I persevered through two years of abuse. Then my husband filed for divorce. It turned out he had been seeing someone else, although I had no clue.

It was difficult for me to take John to his dad's house after the divorce. My ex-husband remarried, and my son witnessed the abuse to his second wife. My mother had instilled a strong faith in the Lord in me at a young age, so I told John, "We need to pray for your daddy. He needs to know Jesus." Through all of this I never gave up, and I think that stemmed from a childhood experience.

When I was three years old, I contracted spinal meningitis, and for 11 years I was ill. When I went outside to play, I would often become physically ill. When I ran inside and told my mother, she called the doctor, and I ended up getting a shot and being sent to bed. Over time I mentally and emotionally learned to press through the illness. I learned to never give up. When I became ill, I went behind a building, threw up, and came back to whatever I was doing as if nothing had happened. Later on I realized that God used difficult circumstances in my life for His glory.

I was shy, but thanks to the presidential physical fitness program, I was discovered in high school. I finished in the top percentile of all girls in the US in several events. As a result my gym teacher put me in basketball, volleyball, and track. At the 1968 Olympics I was awarded a gold medal in the 800 meter, the only American women to win this event. I was only 20 years old and a sophomore in college.

I married in 1969 and began running again to get out my anger. I was angry at myself for marrying that good-looking football player who said, "You'll never make it again as a runner." I was mad at other people—nobody seemed to care about me. I was mad at God—and I wasn't running for Jesus this time. I fell into a deep depression.

Once again, though, I never gave up. After all, I had my son, John—I had to keep going for his sake. At the 1972 Olympics I won a silver medal in the 4-by-400-meter relay. I pulled a muscle in my leg just before that race and ended up running in pain. A scary experience occurred in Munich. The US women's track and field dormitory was directly adjacent to the Israeli dorm where the Israeli athletes were attacked by the Black September terrorist group. When the attack began, we ran for the door to take refuge, but found ourselves locked out. Finally one of our girls, a shot putter, was able to open the door and get us back to safety. But sadness hovered over those Olympic Games and, personally, I was a volcano about to explode.

To come out of a deep depression requires a journey—often a long mental one. I was able to make that journey in spite of all the enemy threw at me, and by the grace of God I was still here. As a single parent, I went back to college and finished my BS in sociology. I accepted my dream job at the Salvation Army, working with inner-city kids. It helps to get away from your own problems when you give to others. I loved the opportunities I had to make a difference in these kids' lives. I participated in the 1976 Olympics and had the honor of being inducted into the US National Track and Field Hall of Fame.

Today my ex-husband has turned his life over to Jesus, thanks to John, and he is a totally different man. He said to me, "John is an incredible young man. I wish I would've raised my kids the way you raised him, and I'm thankful he's back in my life again."

Today I enjoy a career as a sports chaplain, motivational speaker, and gospel singer. I am president of the US Council for Sports Chaplaincy and am pioneering an opportunity for sports chaplains to be credentialed as professionals. I had the honor of being a sports chaplain for the 2012 Olympics in London. I'm also team chaplain for the WNBA team, Tulsa Shock, and a sports chaplain at my church. I am working on my DMin and married to my wonderful husband, Roderick. Today I journal, talk to the Lord, and thank Him for all the blessings He has brought into my life. The road I have walked, or should I say run, has allowed me to be sensitive and to empathize with those individuals brought to me through my ministry.

⤚ WORDS FROM JEENIE ⤙

As Madeline indicates, her husband slapping her prior to their wedding was a red flag for abusive behavior, as was his comment, "I've got you now. You'll never need to be around your friends and family anymore." It practically screamed that more abuse was on the way. Her husband filing for divorce freed her to return to her love of sports and the Olympics in which she excelled, as well as earn a BS degree, have a fulfilling career, and later work on her DMin.

The story is told of Prime Minister Winston Churchill of Great Britain. He was a magnificent statesman who guided his country during World War II. In his elder years, he was invited to a prestigious American university to give the graduation address. The audience was hushed in the presence of such nobility and desired to savor every word. Walking up the podium, he began his speech, "Never, never, never, never, never give up." At that point, he turned, walked to his seat, and sat down. For a few seconds, silence reigned, then with one accord the entire audience stood to their feet with thunderous applause. They got the message. Persevere, no matter what.

In childhood Madeline learned the value of perseverance, pressing on, and endurance during the hardships of dealing with spinal meningitis. Her unwillingness to give in eventually carried her to the Olympic stage. In time, God brought another husband to her who supported her athletic and professional pursuits, encouraging her to be the best she could be. That is true love.

Not many stories have such a unique and exciting ending. However, God's plan for each of us is distinctive and exceptional. Perfect.

> *You will go out in joy*
> *and be led forth in peace;*
> *the mountains and hills*
> *will burst into song before you,*
> *and all the trees of the field*
> *will clap their hands* (Isaiah 55:12).

Marigold often finds herself breaking into song and realizes that God used the abuse in her life so that she can now help others.

A RESTORED LIFE
MARIGOLD

The first time I caught myself breaking into song, I was cooking breakfast. The spontaneous melody astonished me. Sure, I'd sung alone in my home before, but it had always been a conscious decision. Now, in an atmosphere of peace and safety, my grateful heart lifted praise to God while my conscious thoughts supervised oatmeal preparation.

My emotions were unfolding from their longtime fetal position. I'd finally filed for legal separation because of Argyle's mishandling of our finances, but being free from crazy-making talk and other abusive behaviors brought blessed relief to every other area of my life too. I no longer had to retreat to a back bedroom to escape the blare of violent TV programs. I could express audible joy and gratitude without being ridiculed or weighed down by oppressive negativity. My troublesome physical symptoms had subsided. I now had a new job to support myself and build up a little emergency fund.

I was still stung by criticism, however, for not putting a stop to the verbal, emotional, financial, and mental abuse many years before. At least one person said I must have enjoyed the abuse to have stayed so long. Didn't people realize I'd been taught that God expected me to put up with it "till death do us part"? Did they have any idea how difficult breaking free had been? I still felt some people blamed me for failing to cure my husband's mental illness and fix our marriage. Did I need purple bruises or broken bones to convince them of my oppressive, unsafe living environment?

Often I'd sit next to a cozy fire with a mug of tea in my hands and pour my heart out to God. "Why, Lord?" I asked through tears. "Why did You allow me to become trapped in an abusive marriage, and why didn't You answer my desperate prayers for healing?"

I'd always worried about what people thought. Argyle had played that weakness with finesse. Plenty of counselors and authoritative books had said, "Stop worrying about what others think," but it wasn't that easy. I'd been taught all my life to worry about other people's opinions. What people thought of me was somehow connected to my responsibility not to cause them to stumble.

If they did stumble because of anything I had done, or failed to do, I was sternly warned that God would hold me responsible. I could also quote all the verses commanding obedience and submission to my husband, but was less aware of the ones assuring me that my husband's duty was to protect and care for me tenderly.

My anguished prayers for healing were answered in a way I never expected—through a legal separation—and I was prepared to remain in that nebulous marital state for the rest of my life. But four years after the legal separation was finalized, Argyle filed to change it to a divorce. I now found myself a member of a group of people that all my life I'd seen treated as second-class Christians.

In the process, I lost much of what mattered to me: my marriage, ministry, and career, along with my reputation, income, and retirement savings. I also lost my in-laws— precious people who had been my family for more than 30 years. Even though I no longer had to endure the former day-to-day stress, I still felt sidelined, abandoned, and crushed.

But God Himself never left me. Eventually He led me to a church where no one knew me or my history. After the pastor learned my story, he allowed me to sit in the pew and heal with no expectations of public ministry until I was ready.

It has been a decade now since my life imploded. I have recovered in many ways. I realize Scripture verses were taken out of context to indoctrinate me to accept the abuse instead of stand up to it. I'm much more compassionate and full of grace toward others now. I read the Bible with a new perspective. Recognizing how I was taught to rescue my husband from the natural consequences of his behavior enables me to minister to others caught in similar situations.

While God did not cause my difficult circumstances, He is bringing much good out of my painful experience. And now I'm no longer surprised to hear myself break into spontaneous song. It's my spirit's way of expressing the joy of a restored life.

❧ WORDS FROM JEENIE ❧

It's amazing how life can take on a new glow when we are able to move on and away from abuse. Marigold described the peace she felt in her life, which must have truly been a freeing experience.

Even though she separated herself from her husband's abuse, others made accusing and painful comments. They cut deeply. Sadly, responses often seem to be more prevalent among Christians, who sometimes shoot their wounded.

During my painful, unwanted, and impending divorce, one church member said, "Have you prayed about it?" I quietly answered, "Yes." However, I wanted to say, "I have sobbed, fallen on the floor, walked the floors all night without sleep, not eaten, wanted to die, and cried out to God in my desperation and despair." But, it would not have mattered. People make up their minds for whatever reasons, and truth often has no bearing.

"What will people think" permeates my counseling office almost daily. Saying, "Stop it, get on with life, get over it" is insufficient, fruitless, and heartless. And it's easier said than done. Most of the time, I find the feelings are deeply rooted in early childhood. As we slowly and tenderly uncover the roots, healthy thoughts gradually begin to emerge. Work needs to be accomplished at a snail's pace in order to be effective. Even though a fragment may continue to exist, it ceases to have a controlling or debilitating effect on one's life.

Several years after my divorce, I was involved in an automobile accident on August 16, which could have taken my life. On August 16 (ten years later to the day), the contract was drawn for my first book. It was as if God said, "Look what I've done with your life in ten years."

Jesus Christ is the same yesterday and today and forever! (Hebrews 13:8).

In her book, *Sins of a Father*, Kitty Chappell outlines a three-step process for moving from survivor to overcomer.

STEP ONE: FORGIVENESS—Forgiveness has three parts:
1. We must accept forgiveness from God.
2. We must offer forgiveness to others.
3. We must forgive ourselves.

STEP TWO: ACCOUNTABILITY—We must assume responsibility for our thoughts and actions. How can we obey God if we don't take control of our thoughts?

STEP THREE: GRATITUDE—We must cultivate an attitude of gratitude. We can find blessings in every situation.

Pam and Bill Farrel have a worldwide Christian ministry for couples and families. Pam's story gives insight as to how and why it all began.

THE DECISION POINT
PAM FARREL

Often people ask my husband, Bill, and me why we started Love-Wise ministry and why we have dedicated our lives to helping people with their vital relationships: marriage, family, and God. The best answer I can give is, I was rescued from danger and that drives me to try to rescue others by empowering them to courageously believe God has something better for them too.

I was the oldest child in my family. I had a father who loved me deeply and often sacrificed greatly for me, especially financially, but who had pain deep in his heart. He chose to answer that pain with alcohol rather than with a relationship with God. Living with Dad was a Dr. Jekyll/Mr. Hyde experience. Dad would lovingly waltz me around the living room, and then a short time later lash out in anger. Domestic violence seemed a way of life behind the closed doors of our home.

When I was eight, Mom's best friend saw the chaos we were living in, and Kathy said, "Afton, why don't you and the kids come to church with me?"

That first Sunday at church, I saw what love looked like. The whole room was filled with people like Kenny and Kathy, and I wanted what they had! In Sunday School, I memorized Psalm 23, and they gave me a little cross that glowed in the dark. I thought it was the coolest thing I ever saw, so I pinned that cross to my bedroom bulletin board.

One night Dad was drunk and in a rage again, and my sweet mom was trying to talk him down. Things got pretty heated, so I pulled my brother and sister into my room, pushed the dresser in front of the door so Dad couldn't get in, and tucked us all into my bed. When I shut off the light, there in the pitch-black room was that little cross, glowing in the dark.

I silently prayed, *Jesus, when I grow up, I don't want to have a house like this, full of fear, chaos, and craziness. I want to have a home like Kathy's—full of love. Our pastor tells me You are stronger than anything, and I believe that, so please come into my heart, make me into the kind of woman who can marry a great man. PS. God, if You could work it out, I'd love to marry a pastor someday.*

I believe God heard both those prayers of that little girl's heart.

A short while later, Mom also prayed and asked Christ to come into her life, and we both grew in our relationships with God. We learned enough the next couple of years to have the strength to deal with life after a move to a new small town. We lived just a quarter mile from my grandparents, which was a huge blessing because any time things got too volatile, we three kids ran to Grandma and Grandpa's.

In spite of his drinking, Dad got a promotion, and we moved to California. There things got much, much worse.

We found another small evangelical church, and Mom and us kids once again went each Sunday. Dad was hostile toward religion, but he always watched Billy Graham on TV. I think he wanted to change, but he didn't want it bad enough to face down his shame, pain, or guilt and do something to get help.

One day after church, Mom got up her courage to talk with the pastor. After explaining that we would be headed home to a drunk, violent, belligerent man, the pastor simply asked, "So what did you do to make him so mad?" Then he advised Mom to go home and "play nice" and submit.

Mom didn't share this with me until my own husband, ten years later, became a pastor. She begged, "Never give that kind of advice to a woman imprisoned in her own home."

A friend, appropriately named Grace, invited me to a Bible study, and there I met a mentor who poured everything she knew about God into my life. I spent three years writing down everything I could find in the Bible about God being a Father so I could learn to trust men again and so I could learn to recognize a healthy man. I became a leader in my college ministry (then called Campus Crusade), and at a leadership conference, I met the amazing, godly, peace-loving man who is now my husband, Bill.

Shortly after I met Bill, my sister called, frantic. "Dad punched a hole in the wall next to Mom's head. She has bruises from where he held her against the wall."

"I'm on my way home," I said trying to reassure her. I didn't know what I was going to do. I was just 19, 5 feet 2, and all of 100 pounds, but I knew something had to be done.

While I was driving home, Mom's Al-Anon friend and my sister went with Mom to her physician. He said, "I have seen women my entire practice in your situation, and I'll be honest with you about your choices. You can, (1) stay and your husband will likely kill you; (2) stay and you will snap mentally, and you might kill him; or (3) you can take yourself and your kids and get out. Invite your husband to seek help for his addictions, and maybe, if he gets clean and sober, there might be a slim chance of saving this family."

When I arrived home, with the three of us kids standing next to her, she called my grandparents and told them exactly how bad things were and asked if we could all move home and live with them, at least for a while to see if Dad would straighten himself out.

Mom, my sister, my brother, and I moved to Grandma and Grandpa's. God met us as we unpacked the U-Haul. We also unpacked the emotional baggage of our lives, and over the next several years, we all gained ground emotionally and spiritually. We came to a safe, sane, serene, and stable place.

I married, and together Bill and I decided we wanted to dedicate our lives to helping others come to the intersection of love and wisdom, so we write books, speak all over the world, and minister in churches holding out God's redeeming love to any who are looking for the best relationships can offer.

Just recently, on the day of my middle son's wedding, Mom and I had one more errand to run, and as we drove into the Walmart parking lot, "Amazing Grace" was playing on the radio. We sat in the car together crying, worshipping, and holding each other. It was a holy moment of clarity as God reminded us both of His amazing grace and how He empowered us to step into that grace and into a new life. In doing so, our whole family legacy shifted from darkness to God's wondrous light.

~ WORDS FROM JEENIE ~

God can, and does, bring beauty out of ashes. From Pam's painful upbringing, she has chosen with her husband to minister to families in crisis.

I've seen many clients who grew up in childhood abuse and as adults tended to live in the past, thus continuing the cycle of victimization. Likewise, many marry an abuser, and the chain of abuse continues—generation after generation.

As a child, Pam reached out to Christ and accepted Him as her Savior. She had faith to believe this would not always be her lifestyle, but she would someday be freed. Her decision was to marry a good man and establish a home without chaos, fear, and craziness. Later in life she broke out of the bondage, and by doing so has been able to minister to others in need.

Pam stated her father loved her deeply, but he had a pain within him. Likely in order to live with himself, he needed to dull his pain. Alcohol did the trick. Even as a child, Pam was aware of her daddy's internal emotional trauma but was helpless.

Children want to see their fathers as the one who loves, protects, and provides. However, generally those qualifications are seldom present in an abuser. As Christians, abused adult children must detach from the erroneous childhood correlation between their human father and their heavenly Father. When that is accomplished, their trust can be in a God who will never leave nor forsake.

THE BUTTERFLY
SHARYN SUE MCDONALD

Deep within the dark womb of change
Restless in her isolation
Longing for a glimpse of light, she waits.
Freedom eludes her.
Solitary, yet not alone,
Surrounded by darkness, though encased in light,
She is a prisoner of momentary boundaries
Set by unseen hands.
Yearning to be free she questions, "Why?"
Tears fall freely from eyes blinded by self,
Unable to see beyond what is, to what will be.
The miracle begins with a tiny spark.
Cold darkness begins to glow softly.
Warmth flows, life renews,
Releasing the captive heart
From the chrysalis that encased it.
The flame grows brighter.
Hope flickers and ignites within her soul.

Gossamer wings replace the dingy gray of self.
Patterns of color swirl and dance,
Transforming her to a creature of
    exquisite beauty,
Created to be loved.
The faint music of heaven grows stronger.
Glorious melodies flood her senses.
Strength flows through unfurling wings
As she rises on the winds of dawn,
To the One who gently whispers her name,
He waits with strong arms ready to enfold her.
Radiant with love, He tenderly watches her
    draw near.
He smiles and reaches out with
    nail-pierced hands.
And the dance of heaven begins once more.

REFLECTION: Have you moved from a survivor to an overcomer?
Thank God now for helping you to accomplish this.

PRAYER: *Lord, I praise You for restoring my heart, mind, and soul. I am at peace. I rejoice in Your love as I commit my life to You. In Jesus' name I pray, amen.*

APPENDIX

"Domestic violence is the willful intimidation, physical assault, battery, sexual assault, and/or other abusive behavior perpetrated by an intimate partner against another. It is an epidemic affecting individuals in every community, regardless of age, economic status, race, religion, nationality or educational background."

—NATIONAL COALITION AGAINST DOMESTIC VIOLENCE (NCADV.ORG)

"Domestic abuse is a pattern of coercive control that may be primarily made up of psychological abuse, sexual coercion, or economic abuse, that is punctuated by one or more acts of frightening physical violence, credible threat of physical harm, or sexual assault."

—LUNDY BANCROFT (LUNDYBANCROFT.COM)

"Intimate partner violence (IPV) is a serious, preventable public health problem that affects millions of Americans. The term "intimate partner violence" describes physical, sexual, or psychological harm by a current or former partner or spouse. This type of violence can occur among heterosexual or same-sex couples and does not require sexual intimacy."

—CENTERS FOR DISEASE CONTROL AND PREVENTION (CDC.GOV)

FACTS ABOUT DOMESTIC VIOLENCE

- One in every 4 women will experience domestic violence in her lifetime.

  Source: Patricia Tjaden and Nancy Thoennes, National Institute of Justice and the Centers for Disease Control and Prevention, *Extent, Nature and Consequences of Intimate Partner Violence: Findings from the National Violence Against Women Survey,* 2000.

- An estimated 1.3 million women are victims of physical assault by an intimate partner each year.

  Source: Centers for Disease Control and Prevention, National Centers for Injury Prevention and Control, *Costs of Intimate Partner Violence Against Women in the United States,* 2003.

- Eighty-five percent of domestic violence victims are women.

  Source: Bureau of Justice Statistics Crime Data Brief, *Intimate Partner Violence, 1993–2001,* February 2003.

- Historically, females have been most often victimized by someone they knew.

  Source: US Department of Justice, Bureau of Justice Statistics, *Criminal Victimization, 2005,* September 2006.

- Females who are 20 to 24 years of age are at the greatest risk of nonfatal intimate partner violence.

  Source: US Department of Justice, Bureau of Justice Statistics, *Intimate Partner Violence in the United States,* December 2006.

- Most cases of domestic violence are never reported to the police.

  Source: I. H. Frieze and A. Browne, "Violence in Marriage," in L. E. Ohlin and M. H. Tonry, eds., *Family Violence* (Chicago: University of Chicago Press), 1989.

RED FLAGS FOR ABUSIVE BEHAVIOR

Victims of abuse do not cause violence. The abuser is responsible for every act of abuse committed.

The Web site for the Alabama Coalition Against Domestic Violence (acadv.org) signals the following red flags in a potentially abusive relationship (the existence of any one of these alone may not be a clear indicator of an unhealthy relationship; however, one or more of these combined is concerning and deserves further consideration about the relationship dynamics):

- Quick involvement—the perpetrator pushes for a commitment or major event to occur very early in the relationship.
- Isolation—the perpetrator begins asking you to spend less time with your friends and family, and more time with him. You end up no longer maintaining close relationships with friends or family members.
- Suggestions for change—the perpetrator has lots of suggestions on how you can improve your appearance, behavior, etc. You begin to make changes solely based on these suggestions.
- Controlling behaviors—the perpetrator influences your decisions on hobbies, activities, dress, friends, daily routines, etc. You begin to make fewer and fewer decisions without the perpetrator's opinion or influence.
- Information gathering and pop-ins—the perpetrator wants to know the specific details of your day and rarely leaves you alone when you are not with him, such as when you are at work or out with friends.
- Any forms of abuse—the perpetrator may use name calling, intimidation, humiliation, shoving, pushing or other forms of abuse to get you to do whatever they want you to do.

These red flags may occur early in the relationship and be explained by the perpetrator as caring or loving behaviors, such as "I just check on you because I miss you," or "I just want what is best for you," or "I just want us to work on our relationship and spend more time together."

WARNING SIGNS OF ABUSE

Before an abuser starts physically assaulting his victim, he typically demonstrates his abusive tactics through certain behaviors. The following are five major warning signs and some common examples.

- **CHARM**

  Abusers can be very charming, engaging, thoughtful, considerate, and charismatic. He may use that charm to gain very personal information about her, and then use that information later to his advantage.

- **ISOLATION**

  Abusers isolate their victims geographically and socially. Geographic isolation includes moving the victim from her friends, family and support system, or moving frequently in the same area and/or relocating to a rural area.

  Social isolation often begins with wanting the woman to spend time with him and not her family, co-workers, or friends or. He will then slowly isolate her from any person who is a support to her. He dictates whom she can talk to, and he may tell her she cannot have contact with her friends or family.

- **JEALOUSY**

  Jealousy is a tool an abuser uses to control the victim. He may accuse the victim of having affairs.

- **EMOTIONAL ABUSE**

  The goal of emotional abuse is to destroy the victim's self-esteem. He blames her for his violence, puts her down, calls her names and makes threats against her. Over time, she begins to believe what he is telling her, and no longer believes she deserves to be treated with respect. She may even begin to blame herself for the violence he chooses. For some survivors of domestic violence, the emotional abuse may be more difficult to heal from than the physical abuse.

- **CONTROL**

  Abusers are very controlled and very controlling people. In time, the abuser will attempt to control every aspect of the victim's life: where she goes, how she wears her hair, what clothes she wears, whom she talks to. He will control the money and access to money. Abusers are also very controlled people. While they appear to go into a rage or be out of control we know they are very much in control of their behavior.

Developed by the San Diego Family Justice Center and available at Family Justice Center Alliance (familyjusticecenter.org).

DOMESTIC VIOLENCE AND PARENTING

- **CONTROL:** Coerciveness is widely recognized as a central quality of battering men, and one of the areas of life heavily controlled by many men who batter is the mother's parenting.
- **ENTITLEMENT:** A man who batters considers himself entitled to a special status within the family, with the right to use violence when he deems it necessary. This outlook of entitlement can lead to selfish and self-centered behavior on his part.
- **POSSESSIVENESS:** Men who batter often have been observed to perceive their partners as owned objects. This possessive outlook can sometimes extend to their children, partly accounting for the dramatically elevated rates of physical abuse and sexual abuse of children perpetrated by batterers, and for the fact that these men seek custody of their children more often than nonbattering fathers do.

Lundy Bancroft, *The Batterer as Parent* (lundybancroft.com)

What is emotional abuse? Emotional abuse always accompanies, and in most cases precedes, physical battering. Targeted, repeated emotional abuse can severely affect the victim's sense of self and of reality. This comprehensive list of emotionally abusive behaviors abusers use against their partners was developed by the San Diego Family Justice Center and can be located at familyjusticecenter.org.

- Abuser makes hostile jokes about the habits and faults of women.
- Ignores the victim's feelings.
- Withholds approval as a form of punishment .
- Yells at the victim.
- Labels the victim with generally insulting terms: *crazy, stupid.*
- Repeatedly delivers a series of insults specific to the victim and designed to inflict maximum psychological damage.
- Repeatedly humiliates the victim in front of family members and others.
- Isolates the victim socially, perhaps geographically as well.
- Blames the victim for all the abuser's troubles and failures.
- Threatens physical violence and retaliation against the victim, children or other family members.
- Puts down the victim's abilities as a mother, lover, worker, etc.
- Demands all the victim's attention and resents the children.
- Tells the victim about his sexual affairs.
- Constantly accuses her of having affairs, even when she does not have the desire or freedom to have affairs.
- Gives the victim the "silent treatment."
- Threatens to abuse the children and/or get custody of them.
- Tells the victim she must stay with him because she needs him and she couldn't make it without him.
- Accuses the victim of being violent if she acts in any way to protect herself.

- Questions her sense of reality.
- Forces economic dependency: He prevents the victim from working—either by forbidding her to get a job or by making her life so chaotic that she gets fired—and/or he takes her money.
- Puts down or denies the victim's history, heritage, faith, values.
- Hits the wall, not her, to display his power.
- Breaks personal items that have sentimental value to her as a message that he can break her too.
- Threatens, tortures, or kills her/their pets.
- Threatens suicide if the victim doesn't stay with him or do what he wants.
- Spends hours cleaning guns or knives in front of the victim.
- Threatens to kill her or her children.
- Destroys victim's self-esteem.

SAFETY

Safety for the victim and her or their children is the most important thing. Each state has a domestic violence coalition that partners with individual domestic violence programs across the state to provide assistance and safety planning for victims of domestic violence and their children in local communities (see the complete listing of state coalitions here: ncadv.org/resources/StateCoalitionList.php). These programs have advocates on staff who are trained to assist victims with developing individualized safety plans addressing their particular needs and circumstances. To locate an advocate in your area, visit your domestic violence state coalition Web site.

SAFETY PLANNING

From Barbara Hart and Jane Stuehling, 1992. Adapted from *Personalized Safety Plan*, Office of the City Attorney, San Diego, California, April 1990.

A safety plan represents a victim's plan for increasing her safety and preparing in advance for the possibility for further violence. A safety plan recognizes that, although she does not have control over her partner's violence, she does have a choice about *how* to respond to him or her and how to best get herself and her children to safety.

Items to consider when developing a personal safety plan:
STEP 1: Safety during a violent incident.

- If I decide to leave, I will _____
_____ .
(Practice how to get out safely. What doors, windows, elevators, stairwells, or fire escapes would you use?)
- I can keep my purse and car keys ready and put them (place) _____ in order to leave quickly.
- I can tell _____ about the violence and request that they call the police if they hear suspicious noises coming from my house. I can also tell _____ about the violence and request that they call the police if they hear suspicious noises coming from my house.
- I can teach my children how to use the telephone to contact the police and the fire department.
- I will use _____ as my code word with my children or my friends so they can call for help.
- If I have to leave my home, I will go _____
_____ . (Decide this even if you don't think there will be a next time.)

- If I cannot go to the location above, then I can go to _____ or _____ .
- I can also teach some of these strategies to some/all of my children.
- When I expect we are going to have an argument, I will try to move to a space that is lowest risk, such as _____ . (Try to avoid arguments in the bathroom, garage, kitchens, near weapons, or in rooms without access to an outside door.)
- I will use my judgment and intuition. If the situation is very serious, I can give my partner what he or she wants to calm him or her down. I have to protect myself until I or we are out of danger.

STEP 2: Safety when preparing to leave. Leaving must be done with a careful plan in order to increase safety. Batterers often strike back when they believe that a victim is leaving a relationship.

I can use some or all of the following safety strategies:

- I will leave money and an extra set of keys with _____ so I can leave quickly.
- I will keep copies of important documents or keys at _____ .
- I will open a savings account by _____ , to increase my independence.
- The domestic violence program's hotline number is _____ . I can seek shelter by calling this hotline.
- I will check with _____ and _____ to see who would be able to let me stay with them or lend me some money.
- I can leave extra clothes with _____ .

- I will sit down and review my safety plan every _____ in order to plan the safest way to leave the residence. _____ (domestic violence advocate or friend) has agreed to help me review this plan.
- I will rehearse my escape plan and, as appropriate, practice it with my children.

Step 3: Safety in my own residence. It may be impossible to do everything at once, but safety measures can be added step by step. Safety measures I can use include:

- I can change the locks on my doors and windows as soon as possible.
- I can replace wooden doors with steel/metal doors.
- I can install security systems including additional locks, window bars, poles to wedge against doors, an electronic system, etc.
- I can purchase rope ladders to be used for escape from second-floor windows.
- I can install smoke detectors and purchase fire extinguishers for each floor in my house/apartment. I can install an outside lighting system that lights up when a person is coming close to my house.
- I will teach my children how to use the telephone to call me and to call _____ (friend/ clergy/other) in the event that my partner takes the children.
- I will tell people who take care of my children the names of those persons who have permission to pick up my children, and that my partner is not permitted to do so. The people I will inform about pick-up permission include:

_____

(school), (day-care staff), (babysitter), (religious school teacher), (teacher), and (others).

- I can inform (neighbor), (clergy), and (friend) that my partner no longer resides with me and they should call the police if my partner is observed near my residence.

Step 4: Safety on the job and in public. Friends, family, and co-workers can help to protect victims. Victims should consider carefully which people to invite to help secure safety.

I might do any or all of the following:

- I can inform my boss, the security supervisor and _____ _____ at work of my situation.
- I can ask _____ to help screen my telephone calls at work.
- When leaving work I can _____
- When driving home, if problems occur I can _____ _____.
- If I use public transportation I can _____.
- I can use different grocery stores and shopping malls to conduct my business and shop at times that are different from my usual pattern.
- I can use a different bank and take care of my banking at hours different from those I used when residing with my battering partner.
- I can also _____.

Things I might consider taking with me when I leave:
* Identification for myself
* Children's birth certificates
* My birth certificate
* Social Security cards
* School and vaccination records
* Money

* Checkbook, ATM card
* Credit cards
* Keys (house/car/office)
* Driver's license and registration
* Medications
* Welfare identification
* Work permits
* Green card
* Passport(s)
* Divorce papers
* Medical records for all family members
* Lease/rental agreement, house deed, mortgage payment book
* Bank books
* Insurance papers
* Small saleable objects
* Address book
* Pictures
* Jewelry
* Children's favorite toys and/or blankets

LEGAL

There are civil and criminal remedies available for persons who have experienced domestic violence or abuse. In fact, it is not unheard for a survivor of domestic violence to be involved in several legal proceedings at once if:

- a protection order exists (civil);
- criminal charges are pending against the abuser; and
- the survivor is married and seeking a divorce and/or custody of children (civil).

A **protection order** is a civil court order that provides legal protection for someone who is being abused.

It is ideal for survivors of domestic violence to be represented by an attorney in protection order and/or divorce and custody proceedings, however, it is not required. Many communities have legal services/legal aid offices, volunteer lawyer programs, and domestic violence legal clinics that provide free civil legal assistance to victims of domestic violence.

To learn what legal resources are offered in your area, consult the Web site for the state bar association, your state's domestic violence coalition, or the Legal Services Corporation at lsc.gov.

When you speak with an attorney, do not hesitate to ask if the lawyer is experienced in assisting domestic violence victims.

When you meet with an attorney, you should be prepared to provide the following:

- Biographical information for you, your spouse, and your children, including birthdates, Social Security numbers, employment history
- Financial information—in addition to your monthly expenses, a listing of the items owned by you, or you and your spouse (checking and savings accounts, pensions, 401Ks, homes, automobiles), as well as a listing of your debts (credit cards, mortgages, etc.)
- Relevant information from other court cases—if you applied for a protection order, or if there are police reports stemming from abusive incidents during the marriage

Additional legal resources:
Divorce: http://www.legalmomentum.org/assets/pdfs
/divorce_final_2008.pdf

RESOURCES

National Domestic Violence Hotline 1-800-799-SAFE (7233)

SUGGESTED READING

The Batterer as Parent: Addressing the Impact of Domestic Violence on Family Dynamics by Lundy Bancroft

Getting Free: You Can End Abuse and Take Back Your Life by Ginny NiCarthy

Into the Light: A Guide for Battered Women by Leslie Cantrelli

It's My Life Now: Starting Over After an Abusive Relationship or Domestic Violence by Meg Kennedy Dugan and Roger Hock

Keeping the Faith: Guidance for Christian Women Facing Abuse by Marie Fortune

Not to People Like Us: Hidden Abuse in Upscale Marriages by Susan Weitzman

Refuge: A Pathway Out of Domestic Violence and Abuse by Det. Donald Stewart (Out of print)

Should I Stay or Should I Go? A Guide to Knowing If Your Relationship Can—and Should—Be Saved by Lundy Bancroft

The Verbally Abusive Relationship: How to Recognize It and How to Respond by Patricia Evans

When Dad Hurts Mom: Helping Your Children Heal the Wounds of Witnessing Abuse by Lundy Bancroft

When Love Goes Wrong: What to Do When You Can't Do Anything Right by Ann Jones and Susan Schechter

Why Does He Do That? Inside the Minds of Angry and Controlling Men by Lundy Bancroft

Wounded by Words: Healing the Invisible Scars of Emotional Abuse by Susan Titus Osborn, Karen Kosman, and Jeenie Gordon

WEB SITES

National Coalition Against Domestic Violence: ncadv.org
National Center on Domestic and Sexual Violence: ncdsv.org
National Network to End Domestic Violence: nnedv.org
Battered Women's Justice Project: bwjp.org/bwjp_home
Domestic Abuse Intervention Programs: theduluthmodel.org
Futures Without Violence: futureswithoutviolence.org
National Resource Center on Domestic Violence: nrcdv.org
Praxis International: praxisinternational.org
Family Justice Center Alliance: familyjusticecenter.org
Alabama Coalition Against Domestic Violence: acadv.org
Lundy Bancroft: lundybancroft.com

New Hope® Publishers is a division of WMU®, an international organization that challenges Christian believers to understand and be radically involved in God's mission. For more information about WMU, go to wmu.com. More information about New Hope books may be found at NewHopeDigital.com. New Hope books may be purchased at your local bookstore.

Use the QR reader on your
smartphone to visit us online at
NewHopeDigital.com

If you've been blessed by this book, we would like to hear your story. The publisher and author welcome your comments and suggestions at: newhopereader@wmu.org.

RESOURCES FOR ENCOURAGEMENT IN
Your Journey to Healing

Clothed with Power
A Six-Week Journey to Freedom, Power, and Peace
JENNIFER KENNEDY DEAN
ISBN-10: 1-59669-373-8 • ISBN-13: 978-1-59669-373-9
N134114 $14.99

Stronger Still
A Woman's Guide to Turning Your Hurt into Healing for Others
EDNA ELLISON
ISBN-10: 1-59669-090-9 • ISBN-13: 978-1-59669-090-5
N074139 $14.99

A Woman Who Hurts, A God Who Heals
Discovering Unconditional Love
ELSA KOK
ISBN-10: 1-56309-950-0 • ISBN-13: 978-1-59669-335-7
N124142 $14.99

Available in bookstores everywhere.
For information about our books or authors,
visit NewHopeDigital.com.
Experience sample chapters, podcasts, author interviews and more!

NEW HOPE
PUBLISHERS
Gospel-Centered. Missions-Driven.

WorldCrafts^{SM} develops sustainable, fair-trade businesses among impoverished people around the world. Each WorldCrafts product represents lives changed by the opportunity to earn an income with dignity and to hear the offer of everlasting life.

Visit WorldCrafts.org to learn more about WorldCrafts artisans, hosting WorldCrafts parties and to shop!

WORLDCRAFTS^{SM}

Committed. Holistic. Fair Trade.

WorldCrafts.org 1-800-968-7301

WorldCrafts is a division of WMU®.